America's
Unseen Kids

America's Unseen Kids

Teaching English/Language Arts
in Today's Forgotten High Schools

Harold M. Foster
Megan C. Nosol

Foreword by Kylene Beers
Afterword by Robert E. Probst

HEINEMANN
Portsmouth, NH

212908738   5-5-08

Heinemann
361 Hanover Street
Portsmouth, NH 03801–3912
www.heinemann.com

Offices and agents throughout the world

© 2008 by Harold M. Foster and Megan C. Nosol

Cataloging-in-Publication data is on file at the Library of Congress.
ISBN-13: 978-0-325-01060-1
ISBN-10: 0-325-01060-9

Editor: Lisa Luedeke
Developmental editor: Alan Huisman
Production management: Kim Arney
Production coordination: Vicki Kasabian
Cover design: Night & Day Design
Typesetter: Kim Arney
Manufacturing: Steve Bernier

Printed in the United States of America on acid-free paper
12 11 10 09 08 VP 1 2 3 4 5

For Greta, Jane, and Elizabeth.
—Hal

For Łukasz, who reentered my life at the
beginning of the writing of this book and stayed.
You will always be my Irish dream.
And for my loving family—Jim, Sally, Sean, and Keely.
—Megan

Contents

Foreword

The Genteel *Unteaching* of America's Poor

Several years ago, I spent some time observing instruction in a large, inner-city high school. Too many students crowded into too-small classrooms that held too few books and offered too little support of any type created a climate that was at best depressed and at worst was oppressive. Teachers drove daily into a parking lot that was surrounded by an eight-foot cyclone fence with barbed wire looped across the top. The gate into the lot was locked after the last car arrived. Students and teachers entered the fifty-year-old building through front doors that were framed by ten-year-old metal detectors. Hallways were bare except for the occasional poster that reminded students "Truancy Is a Crime" or "A One-Two Punch Is a One-Way Ticket to Suspension." Classrooms all looked the same: worn student desks in long straight rows that were covered in penciled graffiti; battered blackboards that had profanity scratched into them; worn-out overhead projectors that sat on wobbly stools at the center of rooms and projected dimmed images toward screens that hung by dirty cords from ceilings missing tiles; windows covered by broken Venetian blinds; faded green walls that had not been painted in at least a decade and fluorescent lights that sometimes worked, other times did not.

Each day, as students entered the building, security guards instructed them to empty their pockets, empty their backpacks, empty their purses, stand over here for pat downs, hurry up and gather materials, stop pushing, stop yelling, stop cursing, and get to class. At the same time, as teachers entered the main workroom to sign in and retrieve mail from their mailboxes, the principal reminded them how many days remained before *the test*, meaning, of course, the state assessment.

"Make today count," he said each day. "If I walk by your room," he'd remind teachers as they filled Styrofoam cups with coffee from one of three stained Mr. Coffee Makers, "I want to see standards written out on the blackboard and students in their seats and working. In their seats and working." One day, not able to listen to his admonition yet again, I asked if he was serious—that students always needed to be in their desk seats to work.

"Yep," he replied.

"Why?" I asked. "What if they need to be standing up, say, to give a report?"

"Not our kids," he said. "Our kids stay in their seats."

"You're kidding," I said, sure that he was going to break out in a smile, and we'd laugh at his comment.

He stared at me and, with no hint of a smile, not even a grin, explained, "Some kids—those out there heading to class right this minute so they aren't late" he said, nodding toward the bus lot now filled with kids streaming into school, "learn best with rules. Rules and structure. We give it to them." And then he walked away.

He didn't say it unkindly, that comment about "those" kids. With reflection, I realized he said it with sincerity, perhaps concern, and certainly with conviction. Somehow along the way, he had concluded that those kids, *those* kids whose lives are lived in the gaps—the poverty gap, the health care gap, the nutrition gap, to name but a few—and whose lives are spent wondering—wondering where dinner comes from, where they'll sleep tomorrow, what will happen when the rent can't be paid, what they'll do when they're approached about joining a gang, what they'll do when someone in their family is sick and no one can pay for a visit to the doctor, what they'll do when they don't have the bus fare that gets them to the store to buy the poster board for their history report or the novel for English class—*those* kids will do better if we just require that they stay in their seats. *Those* kids just need some structure. And we do them a service, a good service, by giving it to them.

I watched teachers in the building use instructional material that required chanted replies; I saw them distribute photocopied packets that reduced topics such as the Holocaust to a series of literal questions that were to be answered in complete sentences and only in ink, black ink. I asked teachers if they thought classroom discussions might be helpful. All answered no, not for *their* students.

"Those kids, well, they live in such turmoil at home that we provide structure, quiet, orderliness, here at school," one social studies teacher explained to me. An English teacher echoed his sentiments, "Students here need to get the basics; we don't have much time with them when you look at all they need to learn, so we must drill the basics into them. They do better with strong discipline." The science teacher chimed in: "Some kids can handle the higher-level thinking discussions you might see in other schools, but not the kids here; the kids here haven't had anyone show them how to act and so we do. We demand they sit still and answer questions and they learn how to do that."

I looked out into the hallway as students walked past. "Those kids?" I asked. They nodded. "Don't you think they'd enjoy conversation? Discussion? Ideas to debate? Sitting in groups and figuring things out? Trips to the library? Working on a computer?"

One teacher leaned toward me, patted my arm, and interrupted my litany: "You mean well, I'm sure," she said, "but you just don't understand what those kids need. It's a little hard at first," she continued, "but then you realize that those kids, well, they need you to treat them differently if they're going to make good grades."

"Differently from what?" I asked.

She stared at me for a moment before answering, "You know, from other kids, other kids who don't need this type of structured education."

"What type of education do other kids need?" I asked.

She bristled through her smile and said it was obvious to her that some kids could handle the freedom that allowed them to do more creative things, to "handle the higher levels of Bloom's taxonomy," to interact more with their peers, and if I understood more about the students in this high school, I'd understand that.

And there it was—that declaration that those kids, *those* kids whose lives are limited not by their potential and not by their poverty but by the interpretation of what that poverty means they can achieve, require an education that does not look like the education of children whose lives are lived in the security of abundance, or at least the security of enough. That assertion was made with the genteel smile of someone confident that I, too, would see the value of this diminished educational experience once I had spent time with *those* kids.

That declaration has guided too many instructional decisions in too many schools as too many school boards and superintendents and principals and even teachers decide on instructional materials and instructional strategies that, in all likelihood, would not be offered to the gifted kids or the kids whose parents know how to demand of their schools better technology, better libraries, better textbooks, better teachers, better supplies, better tutors, better playgrounds, better gyms, and . . . well, anything that can be bought with the money these parents will willingly, can easily, supply. No one would ever suggest that a scripted program be used to teach these kids; that's the curriculum for *those* kids, because those kids need *that* help, *that* kind of education.

That declaration, that genteel declaration, hides behind the well-intentioned and soft-spoken statements of "they need structure" and "they need discipline" and "they need the basics." That declaration is too easily accepted as wisdom, so we are left with an education of America's poor that cannot be seen as anything more than a segregation by intellectual rigor, something every bit as shameful and harmful as segregation by color.

These are harsh indictments from me, I realize. I also know that many of you holding this book in your hands would never teach any student, especially students of poverty, in such a way. Many of you are as dismayed as I am at the attitudes and comments of the teachers in that high school[1]; many of you believe as I do that this segregation by intellectual rigor under the guise of "helping those kids find some sort of success" is an appalling injustice that must be addressed. For those readers, I am preaching to the choir. But, as a choir director I know and respect once told me, we must preach to the choir because the choir must sing the loudest, sing the best. The choir must lead everyone else, so they must know the most. The choir must get it right, or they will lead the rest astray.

Many of you holding this book in your hands are the choir singing the song of educational reform in your building, in your district, perhaps in your state. You'll want to keep this book, *America's Unseen Kids*, close. In it, authors Hal Foster and Megan Nosol speak boldly—not only about the inequalities that exist in America's schools, but of strategies that allow *those* kids the rich education we want for all students, the rich education each student deserves. In it, they remind us of all that is lost with the genteel unteaching of America's poor.

Kylene Beers
Senior Reading Advisor to Secondary Schools
Teachers College Reading and Writing Project

---

1. I should point out that as I spent more time in the school described in this essay, other attitudes from other teachers emerged. Many believed that the educational experiences that they offered to students at this school were forced on them by district level administrators who in turn felt pressure from state and federal policies. Others eventually reported that they lacked needed knowledge on how to help underachieving students. They explained that while they didn't like what they were doing, they lacked the research base and practical experience to encourage the school administrators or colleagues to use a different approach or to simply use a different approach in their individual classrooms. While I remain dismayed at the number of schools that turn to scripted programs and highly structured class routines—sometimes almost militarist type environments—guided by the belief that "those" kids require an education that is mostly about learning to follow rules, I am always heartened by teachers who stand in opposition to such practices and offer students, all students, rich, exciting, and powerful educational experiences. I find those teachers everywhere—St. Louis, Detroit, Miami, Los Angeles, Houston, New York City, Cleveland, Phoenix, Baton Rouge—and know that they are changing the lives of the students they teach.

Stumbling into a Book

▓ Hal Drags His Feet

The last thing I wanted to do was write a book.

But I thought I might write an article about a collaborative project that I helped create between the university where I teach and a local urban high school which we will refer to in the book as Galway High School. I trotted out my best academic voice and soon discovered that I had no investment in what I was writing. I didn't care about the article, and I didn't know why. With the clear eye of hindsight, I realize now that an article was in no way long enough to capture this ten-year project. Nor was the academic voice I was using able to convey the chaos and stress, our losses and victories, and the unexpected insights we stumbled onto as we explored a possible solution to one of the great dilemmas of American life: teaching at-risk kids.

My experiences were screaming to be turned into something more substantial. After all, the project had been at the center of my life for ten years. It was a collaboration between me, an English educator; my English education students; a great high school English teacher (called Sally Eisenreich here); and her high school students. Bringing my university students into the real world of school kept me inside the boundaries of teaching. I never had to go home at night and say, "Wow, I'm so removed from the real world. What am I going to tell my class tomorrow?" This project made it impossible for me to lie to my students.

Then the city decided to close the high school. They may have needed to close Galway for a good reason, to secure funds to help rebuild the other city high schools. Nonetheless, the collaboration was going to end. At the same time, my career was also coming to an end: I was approaching retirement age. Searching for ways to close all the chapters of my life, I saw the two as mixed. Was I going to spend my last years as an education professor disenfranchised from the real world of the classroom?

I needed closure, but I was afraid of writing something that was not me, a piece of work constructed on someone else's terms. I certainly didn't want to write a book.

Then Megan knocked on my door.

The conversations Megan and I had are how this book came to be. That's the great thing about collaborations: both sides need to compromise, cooperate, relinquish control. Megan is my student, but it was smart of me to listen to her, just as Megan was wise to listen to me. When she recommended that we write about how my stumbling led to this book, I listened. Inexorably, words appeared, chapters emerged, a structure was formed, and this book became a reality.

◼ Megan Speaks Her Mind

I was enrolled in one of the classes that participated in the Galway High School project. It was the first semester of my master's program, and I was also working with Hal outside the classroom as his graduate assistant. We didn't begin with the intention of writing a book. My task was simply to help Hal get information for his article.

Because I was Hal's graduate assistant, I had a different role from the other students in the class. Hal put me in charge of the evaluation committee, which gathered information about Sally's high school students and their personal and academic lives. This assignment became the basis of four case studies we undertook: I purposely matched four college students with four high school students in Sally's class based on what I judged were their compatible personalities and the kind of help I anticipated the college students could provide. I wasn't going to conduct empirical research, but I planned to tell the stories of how these relationships developed.

In the beginning, everything was on track; the case study pairs were creating real relationships.

Then everything started unraveling.

One of the Galway case study students, who had deep emotional and mental issues, disliked her college-student mentor. Another was creating problems for Galway's teachers and administrators and was consequently removed from the class. The evaluation committee had to abandon its two most interesting case studies. The remaining subjects were academically solid, and we quickly ran out of things to learn from them. The case studies came to an untimely end.

Suddenly I had no work to do.

Hal and I started talking about how we could resolve the problems but then decided just to cut our losses. I was lost and disappointed. We walked over to Starbucks, our usual meeting place, to devise a new plan. I reminded Hal that he had spearheaded this project for ten years: we had meaningful data, and we couldn't give up. The project was a big part of his life. He needed closure. I told Hal he should write a book.

■ Hal Thinks, "This Might Work"

Megan turned twenty-three that November 1. My birthday presents to her were the Jon Krakauer book about Everest, *Into Thin Air*, and a rough outline of a book on the collaboration project with specific assignments for her to work on for the month of November. I was hoping this was the focus Megan needed. I still didn't want to do a book, but I felt that Megan's graduate assistantship experience was rapidly falling apart and that once again we needed structure.

Megan and I began writing. She sat at her desk and I sat at mine, each of us putting our memories into words. Before we knew it, we had some pages written, some kind of outline, some vague plans to continue.

The momentum that was beginning to take shape finally came into focus at the National Council of Teachers of English meeting in Pittsburgh, when I ran into my former editor, who expressed interest in the idea of this book. She told me she would be happy to read a prospectus without reading chapters. I thought, "Oh my God, this might work." I knew two things about my writing, whatever it was to become: it was going to be through my eyes, with my voice, my best attempt to re-create the experience for my readers, and it was also going to exhibit the voice of a teacher in training who had participated in the project. There was no way I was going to do this book without Megan.

Much of my enthusiasm for this book stems from my being able to use a new teacher as a voice to reach novice teacher readers. Through Megan, teachers will be able to:

- empathize
- identify
- commiserate
- share
- learn

As a veteran, I have discovered that no experienced teacher can figure out what a new teacher thinks or feels in a classroom. In this book, Megan tells us that, up close and personal.

Megan provides the fresh perspective obtained from experiencing the project for the first time, but she has also spent many hours with me shaping the curriculum, designing and monitoring the case studies, helping with assessment, and running the

Shakespeare unit. She has experienced the stress, the frustration, and the fear of failure along with me. She knows what it means to work hard, reach out to a group of students so different from her in so many ways, connect with them, and teach them lessons for a lifetime. Megan tells her truth here, and sometimes it's painful to read.

The students we worked with at Galway had not been tracked into advanced classes. These were the kids in the middle, the students society brands with low expectations, our invisible students. We have faith that these students can thrive in an enriched, accelerated curriculum. We believe that the only good curriculum is the advanced curriculum, where real writing occurs, interesting and challenging books are read, and students are equipped to think deeply and wisely in preparation for a rigorous college curriculum. No worksheets, no fragmented lessons. This curriculum is intelligent, motivating, and tough.

If teaching were easy, everyone would know how to do it. Therefore, Megan and I enumerate rather than hide all the problems we faced, each from our own point of view. However, we arrive at the same place in the end. This book is primarily about being hopeful and setting high expectations because this curriculum has been a success every single year of the ten-year project. It works, and it can work in any school.

■ Hal Describes the Project

Ten years ago a teacher, whom I'll call Sally, came to my office and asked if I could bring my future English teachers into her classroom. Sally was very interested in training English teachers for urban schools. Since Galway was a short distance from campus, my college class met at Galway, initially working with Sally's students primarily as tutors. However, over the years the project grew to the point where my students took over the class completely; one or two of my students were always present in Sally's Galway classroom and delivered a very carefully planned curriculum, one similar to those taught in advanced English classrooms in the best high schools in the United States. It was writing intensive, it was structured as a reading workshop, and there was a Shakespeare unit at the end. We celebrated the high school students' achievements with an end-of-year party at which their writing was shared and awards were bestowed.

We taught the kids that society found to be "incapable" of doing challenging work. We certainly ran into students who were puzzles we did not solve. But for the most part our "at-risk" high school students (at risk of boredom, low expectations, stereotyping) met the challenge, academically as well as emotionally.

Although college tutors often helped the student teacher who was responsible for the lesson, many times the student teacher was the only adult in this room of between twenty and thirty high school students. We know our curriculum can be taught by a single teacher with a classroom of these at-risk kids. We did it, and we saw Sally do it with her other classes.

Many teachers do discover these kids and set them on the path of a productive life, but many of these kids remain invisible. They have to be found, challenged, and given the skills they need to achieve productive lives. To that end, this book describes the curriculum we developed and continue to develop, and it describes many of the high school students we encountered and their learning issues. All the stories we tell are true. Therefore, the book is not just about success but also about the challenges we face.

Incredibly, the project did not die with the closing of Galway. Sally transferred to a school a short drive from our campus, and we were able to continue the project at the new school. As I write this, we are completing our second year there, and it is going very well. We may also have identified a teacher in Sally's school, a project veteran who chose to stay in city schools, to continue working with us when Sally retires. So for the near future, much to my surprise and delight, we can still impact future English teachers and these wonderful kids we encounter.

But my biggest hope is that this book will help reinforce what many of you already know: sometimes we make hurtful judgments about kids that are not true and that often create great harm and hopelessness. With the right teachers and the right approaches, some long-range planning, and a more thought-out curriculum delivered early, we can provide decent futures for many more kids than we think possible.

Our Guiding Themes for Teachers of At-Risk Students

(What We Learned from At-Risk Classrooms)

Stop stereotyping.

Respect diversity in culture and language.

Create strong teacher-student relationships.

Hold high expectations.

Implement student-centered teaching.

Give students hope in their ability to read and write.

Connect students' experiences to what they are learning.

Allow students to select what they read and write.

Apply different teaching techniques to appeal to all learning styles.

Deliver an advanced curriculum.

Provide students with ample opportunities to share their work.

Learn to live with complexity.

Celebrate student achievement.

Take advantage of all possible resources.

Reflect on your teaching constantly.

What People on the Outside Don't See

Breaking the Stereotypes

■ The Lowdown on At-Risk and Urban Education

Did you know . . . ?

- Teachers who share the same racial background as their students eliminate or reduce problems related to the institutionalized culture of urban schools (Tyson 2003).
- Research reveals that low socioeconomic status has a negative impact on academic achievement (Kopetz, Lease, and Warren-Kring 2006).
- The number of families living in poverty has increased from 7.2 million in 2002 to 7.6 million in 2003. African Americans have the largest poverty rate at 24.4 percent (Kopetz, Lease, and Warren-Kring 2006).
- Although moving once or twice during the public school years may not be harmful, most research shows that high mobility lowers student achievement—particularly when the students are from low-income, less-educated families ("Highly Mobile Students" 1991, 1).
- Sixty percent of high-income students graduate from college by age 26, but only 7 percent of low-income students graduate from college by age 26 (Kopetz, Lease, and Warren-Kring 2006).
- Fifty percent of Asian Americans, 30 percent of white non-Hispanic Americans, 17.3 percent of African Americans, and 11.4 percent of Hispanic Americans have earned a bachelor's degree by the age of 25 (Kopetz, Lease, and Warren-Kring 2006).

- Graduation rates for students who attend school in high-poverty, racially seg-regated, and urban school districts lag from 15 to 18 percent behind those of their peers (Swanson 2004).
- Based on data for the 2003–04 school year published by the National Assess-ment of Educational Statistics, the rate of above-proficient Caucasian fourth graders is 40 percent in reading and 35 percent in math; the rate of above-proficient African American fourth graders is 12 percent in reading and 5 percent in math; and the rate of above-proficient Hispanic American fourth graders is 16 percent in reading and 10 percent in math (Kopetz, Lease, and Warren-Kring 2006).
- "Nationwide, only about 70 percent of ninth graders make it to graduation four years later. And that figure drops to 46 percent for black males and 52 percent for Hispanic males. About six in 10 black and Hispanic females earn a diploma within four years of entering high school" ("Diplomas Count for What?" 2007, 5).

Megan Wants to Become an English Teacher

I Discover Galway High School

When I walked into Hal's office seeking information about how to obtain a master's in education with licensure (a state teaching license), he was noticeably preoccupied, shuffling things around in his cabinet and on his desk. This made me nervous. I had arrived on campus that day already concerned that as a graduate student I might not get the same level of attention I had received from the English department when I was an undergraduate.

As he went over the degree program with me, he confessed that he was having a bad day. One of his students, who was working with him on a project at Galway High School, had had his car stolen, and all the high school students' writings from the se-mester were in the car's backseat.

Since I had been raised in this city, I was too embarrassed to ask Hal where the school was located. Eventually, I realized I could see the high school from any of my classrooms on campus. For four years, I had parked next to the school in a university parking deck. Some days, I had parked *in* the high school's parking lot, never knowing why I received a ticket. I had most of my classes in the College of Arts and Sciences building, directly across from Galway, but the school had never registered on my per-sonal radar screen. The building did not look like any high school I knew; it was dingy, without windows; it seemed dead. I was used to high schools that were inviting edi-fices with grand entrances and elegant statues.

I Hear Things About Galway

Family members, close friends, and teachers in other school districts all warned me about Galway and its dangerous reputation.

"Of all places, Galway High School?"

"Call me if something bad happens."

"I can reach you in less than five minutes."

"Don't ever walk alone in the halls."

"There are police officers there—use them."

Welcome to Galway High School—a school with chronic absenteeism, teenage pregnancies, drug busts, hall fights, false fire alarms, and called-in bomb threats—where a female police officer was beaten senseless by crazed students in 1995—whose students break out in fights at downtown bus stops and jump students from other schools—where doors are locked to prevent street gangs from getting in—where to get out, you have to find a door without a padlock—where the principals continually roam the hallways, using their walkie-talkies like monitors in a war zone—where students like me would never consider going because Galway High School is a city school in the worst sense of the term.

I love cities. I've been to New York City; Chicago; Washington, DC; Dublin; and London. These are vibrant, exciting, culturally diverse places. However, when people say "city school," what they really mean is this, as defined by the SUNY Oswego School of Education (Russo 2004).

1. The school is located in a city.
2. The school has a large amount of economically disadvantaged students (as measured by free and reduced-price lunch data).
3. The school has a high percentage of students of color.
4. The school has a high percentage of students who are Limited English Proficient.
5. The school has been designated high need or academic emergency by the school district.

Galway High School fits every single one of the above criteria.

1. The high school is located on the edge of downtown, surrounded by warehouses, with its back to the university.
2. Out of its 860 students, 521 are eligible for free lunches, and 43 are eligible for reduced-price lunches (National Center for Education Statistics 2005).
3. Some 645 students are black, 144 white, 34 Asians or Pacific Islanders, and 26 Hispanic (National Center for Education Statistics 2005).

4. Galway has the only English as a Second Language (ESL) program in its school district.
5. For four of the past five years, Galway has been designated an academic emergency, the lowest rating for school performance in the state (Ohio Department of Education 2005).

For most people, Galway High School is invisible; it doesn't exist. When you put the word *school* after *city*, it doesn't mean Times Square, art galleries, beautiful parks—it means decay, low expectations, and discipline problems. It means a school where the worst teachers are warehoused, where there are few resources and limited opportunities, and where there are large numbers of poor, minority students.

I Experience Galway

As I walked with my college peers through the halls on the first day of my participation in the project, I expected to be in another world—and not a good one, from all the warnings I had been given. What I saw, however, didn't seem that different from what I had encountered in the halls of my Catholic high school: rowdy teenagers stopping by the lockers of their friends to chat and racing to get to their next classes before the bell rang.

Yet the moment I walked into the classroom I would be working in, I knew I was in an unfamiliar place. I saw kids with blank looks and others with their heads down on their desks. Several boys and girls chatted back and forth, while other kids talked on their cell phones. I quickly realized the class was extremely diverse. The kids were mostly African American, but there were a few Asian, Latino, and Caucasian students. My college class was made up of Caucasians and one African American.

We college students were diverse in a different way. There were a couple of older, nontraditional students and a mix of undergraduate and graduate students. Most of us had come from public high schools, one was an ESL student (and an alumnus of Galway), and then there was me . . . a white, Catholic-school girl.

The differences setting the college students apart from the high school students were easy to see: culture, age, generation. Communication was slow and awkward. We were afraid of them; they were afraid of us. That first day, we participated in a warm-up activity meant to encourage the college and high school students to mingle. Instead, everyone stuck to their peer groups.

The real talking wouldn't begin for seven weeks.

The Urban High School Student I Never Imagined

Emily was the easiest student for me to reach. Emily was motivated. She had dreams of going to college. She was encouraged by her teachers and parents. She wanted to run track in college, and I had played college soccer. She wanted my guidance on how to get into a Division I athletic program. Emily and I were a natural fit.

Emily was also a voracious reader—at least one book a week. When the college tutors asked for volunteers to read their autobiographies to the class, Emily was the first to raise her hand. Not only was her paper organized and well structured, her writing was also vivid and powerful. Emily participated in two sports, was actively involved in at least one academic club, and spent many of her afternoons in a future teachers program at a neighboring high school.

While Emily had the support of her parents and teachers, no one had clued her in to the ways of higher education. Emily would be the first person in her family to go to college, and her parents were unaware of financial aid, the admissions process, and college athletics. After talking with her, I realized that she lacked the essential information she needed to achieve her college goals. Although Emily was equipped in every way to succeed in college, she needed some extra attention, which I could give her.

One day, I pulled Emily out of class and took her on a tour of my university. She met people who worked in the financial aid office, toured the college of education, and received information about admissions and programs. I introduced her to the head coach of the university track and field team, and then I took her to lunch in our new student union. She asked me for advice about obtaining scholarships and getting recruited for a Division I track team, and we talked about the things she needed to do to prepare for college—applications, the FAFSA, college essays, and the courses she would probably take her first year. We discussed the importance of preparing for the ACT and keeping up her good grades. I gave her an ACT preparation book with many practice tests and study tips. Emily was excited and grateful for this personal attention.

I am confident that Emily will be successful in college, graduate, and become a great teacher. When people mentioned urban high school students, I couldn't even imagine an Emily. She was more invisible than her classmates because she was a confident, thriving student at Galway who benefited from caring teachers and loving parents. She held realistic dreams and aspirations. Emily's story is not a story of failure. There are many Emilys at Galway High School who flourish. These kids have the potential for a successful future.

The Most Difficult Challenge

Alisha, on the other hand, stole my heart.

She was cold, distant, rude, and intimidating, claiming she "hates white people." She was often absent from class and rarely did her work, and it took a great amount of effort to calm her down because of her emotional and family problems.

Yet, I identified more with Alisha than with Emily.

I was a mediocre student in high school. I was bored with my classes, unmotivated, and subtly discouraged by both my teachers and my parents. I felt no one believed in me, that I didn't have any talents. I did very little work, which was good enough for me at the time. I accepted that I would go to an open-admission state college and wasn't surprised when I got rejection letters from the two private colleges to which I'd applied. My parents tried all kinds of ploys to get me to work harder in school like my brother and sister, who were both good students, but nothing sparked me.

Yet something inside me wasn't satisfied.

It was the summer before my first year at Bowling Green State University. I had just finished the English composition placement test. My mom and I were waiting for the results outside my soon-to-be adviser's office. I was nervous, excited, and even a little confident because I'd been able to write on something I felt strongly about—the death penalty.

My name was called, and my mom and I walked into Mr. Nicholson's office and sat down. He pulled out my writing sample and asked, "Megan, did you take AP English in high school?" I laughed and said no, wondering why he would ask an average student like me that question. He looked me straight in the eye. "I think you belong in our advanced English course here. We are going to sign you up, if that's okay with you." I looked at my mom, thinking, *What in the world is he talking about?* My mom was happy for me and proud of my effort, but I was shocked and surprised when he called me a "great writer." He liked my arguments and my writing style. For the first time, it occurred to me that perhaps I had an academic strength.

After one semester of advanced English, I decided to become an English major. I went from being a run-of-the-mill student to getting straight As. It was that simple but also that complex. Someone, a professor of writing and not my mom, for once, had set high expectations for me, and as a result, I set high expectations for myself because I knew I could do well.

Now it was payback time. It was my turn to set high expectations for Alisha and show her she could be successful in school. This was going to be my first "teachable moment."

Even though Alisha was emotionally unavailable, I made an effort to reach out and say hello to her and let her know I cared about what she was doing in class. I started sitting next to her, getting to know her and slowly building her trust. I told her about myself and about my difficulties in high school. When she told me she was "stupid" and had no friends, I showed her through her own class work that she was capable of writing well. I reassured her I was available when she needed to talk about school or life.

I began to realize that Alisha, one of the most problematic students in the school, and I shared one thing in common. Even though I wasn't a troublemaker in high school and I didn't have complex emotional, family, or learning problems like Alisha did, I related to her apathetic high school experience. I remember my lack of confidence and drive when I was her age. Like Alisha, I felt I had no talents in high school; I needed a teacher who would take the time to see through my quietness and poor self-esteem and help me discover my strengths.

For the rest of the semester, I worked closely with Alisha. I chose a book for her to read based on her interests, helped her with her writing assignments, and encouraged her to show her academic talents. Even though I went to a private school and Alisha was at Galway, we both shared an invisibility that prevented us from reaching our potential.

▪ Hal Reflects on Urban Learning Styles

Urban Schools Like Galway Are Invisible to the Public

Until Megan entered the building, experienced what it was like to teach at Galway High School, and developed relationships with Galway students, she was typical of how people looked at city schools like Galway. After she spent a significant amount of time in the building, going to the same class every day, working with the same students day in and day out, she became an insider, establishing deep teacher-student relationships with complicated and interesting people who happened to be students at Galway. They became so visible that Megan was able to transcend social class and race to identify with the most troubled student that we have encountered in the collaboration project, Alisha. Thus, Megan has taken us on the full journey—from the invisible school, to the perceived school, to the real school. The community surrounding Galway sees only the "urban school" label, as Megan did before she started teaching. After her experiences at Galway, Megan wrote to me, "I hate phrases like 'urban school' and 'urban learning style' now. Teaching at Galway has made me realize the potential negative, limiting connotations of these terms."

At-Risk and Urban Kids and Schools Are Unfairly Stereotyped

There are experts in education who believe that a student's learning style depends on his or her race. For instance, in *Comprehensive Urban Education*, Koptez, Lease, and Warren-Kring (2006) describe four cognitive learning styles:

- accommodator (leader, risk taker, achiever)
- assimilator (planner, theorist, analyst)

- diverger (creator, artist, someone sensitive to values)
- converger (problem solver, deducer, decision maker)

According to these authors, "Hispanics, blacks, and Asians identified themselves most often as assimilators and divergers. Divergers are the least identified learning style of white students, yet the second highest for Hispanics and Asians" (53–54). The authors claim divergers are imaginative, sensitive, and tend to recognize problems. They also argue whites are most likely to be convergers, problem solvers, and deducers, while blacks and Hispanics are least likely to be convergers.

A noted expert in African American education also sees the potential for race-related learning styles. He believes that many black children learn best in the oral tradition. He suggests many black children come from families who value oral literacy skills and enter schools that require a great amount of silent, linear work.

Our cooperating teacher at Galway High School, Sally Eisenreich, has mixed opinions about black kids learning best in the oral tradition. Sally gave me these insights into what may characterize her students and the way they learn.

- They like to express themselves through speaking as a way of learning.
- They need concrete examples that relate to their lives in order to move forward.
- They like to work in teams or at least with another student.

After years of teaching in Galway, however, Sally is absolutely convinced the only two teaching strategies that consistently make a difference with her students are:

1. building strong teacher-student relationships
2. having high expectations

Nothing illustrates how careful a teacher should be with generalities and stereotypes as our experiences with Johnny, an African American student. Johnny was a big, unkempt kid. He came to class and immediately put his head down on his desk, hidden inside his hooded sweatshirt. For the first month, I do not think anyone heard him say a word.

About five weeks into the project, Johnny told his tutor about his music ambitions and the rap poetry he wrote. The tutor read his lyrics with great interest and appreciation. Johnny told her that he first wrote drafts, which he then carefully and meticulously revised. The tutor explained this was exactly what was expected on class assignments. Hesitantly, Johnny began to write for class. When he saw that we weren't judgmental or negative, were interested in what he had to say, and were willing to help him say it in a way that enhanced his writing through revising and editing, he embraced the class.

Johnny was so easily scared that we had to sit next to him and speak softly when we worked with him, but we could see him respond to our encouragement. I cannot begin to describe his learning style and neither can his tutor; he certainly cannot be placed in any of the above categories. With our support, however, he became a stronger reader and writer, as his other teachers reported: "Whatever you are doing with Johnny is working; his writing has improved dramatically." Here was a young man who was so shy and introverted he could hardly speak above a whisper, yet he began to read and perform Shakespeare. Johnny was learning, developing, and growing; we all loved him and he loved us.

In the end, Johnny broke our hearts. On what may have been the worst day ever in any year of this project, I came in and saw Johnny walking back and forth in the classroom. Sally gave me the news that Johnny's mother had to move (maybe she could no longer afford the rent, maybe there was some other reason), and this would be Johnny's last day in our class.

Later that year, I visited Johnny in his new school. I brought him a bag of candy and the portfolio we had created from the writing he left behind. He was happy to see me, and at least I had one more chance to greet this young man who came so far. What could have been. . . .

We Must Learn to Live with Complexity

Experts, scholars, educators—all of them want to give us definite answers on how urban kids learn. The truth is we saw no empirical evidence that supported the generalities we read and were told about urban education and urban learning styles. Megan and I tried to see things that separated Galway from suburban and private schools, but we couldn't find them. Every time we tried, we just got closer to Megan's private-school experience, not further away. It was a surprise to both of us how much Megan identified with the kids at Galway; the parallels are inescapable.

Megan and I learned that the labels don't fit. In some ways it would be nice if they did—it would be easy if we could recognize the urban learning style, develop the lessons, and solve problems. If only. . . .

The more time we spent at Galway, the less "urban" it became. The more we got to know the kids, the less we branded them with the clichés of the "urban, city school" label. And once my college students established these teacher-student relationships, the kids began to learn.

What worked was the exact opposite of what the experts were telling us to do. When we gave up the notion that these students had specific learning styles, we learned how to teach.

We learned to live with complexity.

◼ Hal and Megan Reflect on Urban Education

We are overwhelmed by the bleakness of the urban education statistics. We asked our expert on African American education, Francis Broadway, about them, and he told us stats like these do not tell the whole story. At Galway, we encountered kids whose lives were so complicated that school seemed almost impossible. Yet many of these kids did well and thrived. So maybe a curriculum like ours could make a difference.

However, no project like ours will eradicate these problems quickly. Our schools will need hundreds of projects like these; it will take generations of committed teachers, administrators, and communities and most likely a willingness to allow experimentation and change, something big school bureaucracies find difficult. We don't see how mass standardized testing helps. Wouldn't it be nice if there were plans, efforts, policies—something more than just talk—to change what is one of the most pressing, daunting dilemmas of our educational system?

Hal's generation broke it; Megan's generation will have to fix it. How? What can the current generation do? What kind of school restructuring will work? Can they change the curriculum in a way that will help? What vision of schools do they see that can improve this bleak situation? What have people like Megan learned from this project that could be instituted to solve the vexing problems these statistics uncover?

Even though teaching in Galway High School was a wonderful experience for Megan, it also made her angry. We live in one of the richest, most powerful countries in the world, but while she grew up in beautiful private schools, kids like Emily, Alisha, and Johnny are forced to attend run-down, technologically lacking, strapped-for-funds schools like Galway. How can teachers pass kids who are not academically ready for the next grade and who need special attention, like Alisha?

Previous generations of politicians, administrators, educational leaders, and even teachers have allowed problems like this to persist, become the accepted norm, and grow so deep that it makes it hard for anyone who cares about students and their education to dig their way out. Why are eleventh-grade Galway High School students so far behind eighth graders of local suburban schools? Why don't schools use the free resources around them, such as education students at nearby colleges, for tutoring and support?

◼ Megan's Generation's To-Do List

The problem, which involves a mix of racial and economic inequality, is so entrenched it's hard to know where to begin. Here's a list based on what we've seen and experienced that shows what needs to be done to even out the playing field for all students.

- Get parents interested and involved in their children's schooling.
- Stop the media from depicting urban schools like Galway High School as violent, dangerous institutions with talentless, poor kids.
- Get people in power, such as sincere politicians and administrators, to be more proactive and genuine about transforming our nation's public schools into schools that communities and students can be proud of.
- Teach kids what they need to do to get to college and why it is important to go to college—show them how to choose a college, how to fill out the applications, how to get financial aid and help on filling out the FAFSA forms, what they can expect during the first year.
- Prepare kids for their future by bringing more technology into the classroom; we are living in a technologically advanced world.
- Make urban schools equal to the best suburban and private schools in funding, resources, and curriculum.
- Revamp our educational system so that students are taught more than just how to pass our standardized tests.

What We Learned

- Teachers build relationships with students by seeing through stereotypes and getting to know each student personally.
- Once a teacher forms relationships with students, the students will do the work.
- "Real talk" between the teacher and the students begins after seven weeks.
- Teachers need to set high expectations for all students.
- When a teacher sets and reinforces high expectations for students, students will raise their own expectations.

Classroom Activities

1. Hold a discussion with your students about what needs to change in their community to make their school better.
2. Take your students on a tour of a nearby college to show them the basics. Show them how to fill out college applications, get someone from the financial aid department to talk about filling out the FAFSA forms and applying for scholarships, take interested students to the athletic department and have someone talk to them about college athletics and recruitment. If you can't go

on a college tour, have college students come into your class to talk about the college admissions process, financial aid, and college athletics. *It's free!*

3. Get retired citizens or college students to come into your classroom and tutor your struggling students.

4. Develop a mentoring program through which your students can form friendships with knowledgeable college students.

From Rough Draft to Publication

Teaching the Writing Process to Urban Kids

■ Our Core Principles

At the beginning of every semester, the tutors and I see a pattern. We notice that Galway kids:

- have good stories to tell but have trouble conveying their stories in writing
- have difficulty brainstorming ideas
- have interesting, valid arguments but lack the writing tools to articulate them
- don't have strategies to cope with writer's block and organizational problems
- become frustrated by the thought of writing on demand because they have low confidence in their abilities
- write like they speak

With these problems in mind, we have created a writing curriculum that addresses the specific needs of our Galway students. The curriculum changes each semester, but the core principles of our three writing units—autobiography, persuasion, and extended response—stay the same, and tutors stick to them. These principles, based on the ideas of some of the smartest writing teachers in America, such as Donald Graves (1983), Linda Rief (1992), and Tom Romano (2000), are derived from the writing curriculum in *Crossing Over: Teaching Meaning-Centered Secondary English Language Arts* (Foster 2002).

- *Pick meaningful topics.* Students write about things that engage them. Tutors provide a variety of ideas and writing opportunities for students to select from.
- *Give students the freedom to write.* Students, much of the time, are free to write whatever they want without the work being judged. Most student writing remains free and unedited.

- *Allow students to develop their voice and discover meaning.* Students need the freedom to write without inhibition to develop styles and rediscover the meaning and path of their writing. Young writers can do this only without fear of penalty for grammatical and structural errors.
- *Encourage students to develop public statements.* Students select a piece from among their drafts to develop into a published statement for an audience.
- *Respond to student writing.* Students receive responses to their writing from tutors and their peers that help shape and craft the writing into a finished piece.
- *Give lots of editing help.* Students get feedback from tutors to help them edit their public statements into logical, clear, organized, error-free writing.
- *Use technology.* Student writers are given every opportunity to learn how to use word processors and computers as technological tools in the writing process.
- *Maintain flexibility.* Although the composing process may be demonstrated as a method or paradigm, all writers and writing needs are different. Thus, tutors need to be careful not to apply a rigid set of guidelines to every writer.

■ Teaching Prewriting and Drafting Through Autobiography

The semester always begins with autobiographical writing, a getting-to-know-you piece that the tutors write with the students. This autobiography unit begins the semester because students know more about themselves than anything else; autobiography is the most student-friendly writing. It gives tutors information about the students, such as interests, academic strengths and weaknesses, and career aspirations. It also boosts students' confidence since it's easy for them to write about themselves.

Hands sweat; heartbeats increase; blood pressures rise. The first day of class, when teachers and students meet one another, is one of the most stressful experiences of the school year. It is way too early to build connections; way too early for anything other than an anonymous teacher to begin the slow evolutionary process of teaching English to a group of unknown and undifferentiated students.

Often, Galway students receive a scaffolding sheet with background questions, such as these.

- What is your age?
- When is your birth date?
- Where is your place of birth?
- How was your name chosen?
- What are your favorite things to do?
- What hobbies or hidden talents do you have?

- What magazines do you like?
- What are your favorite childhood movies?
- What TV shows do you watch and why?

These scaffolding sheets are a brainstorming tool. Prewriting is not a science but a craft. With guidance, a little judgment, and a lot of flexibility, the writing begins, tentatively at first, but it definitely begins.

During this unit, we often find out how extraordinary the lives of many of the Galway students are.

- Whisper, a loud newborn, was named in hopes she would quiet down, which she did. Her grandma raised her and would tell her stories about her mom, whom she missed desperately.
- Sammy, a father since tenth grade, works two jobs to help raise his baby. He misses having fun like a normal teenager, "but I have this responsibility and I will do right by it."
- Billy skips school every Tuesday to "go out with his friends" to spend his check from working at Kentucky Fried Chicken.
- Samantha, the only white girl in class, loves school but can't help overhearing racial remarks that hurt. "No offense, of course."
- Artis hopes to own a restaurant some day.

Modeling Writing for Students

Modeling writing introduces students to the idea that writing isn't just for them—teachers write as well. Also, when teachers share drafts, students see that drafts aren't perfect pieces of writing but rather a necessary and creative step toward the development of a piece. Nobody sets down words on paper perfectly the first time; it is hard enough to get words on paper at all. But the most important point about modeling writing is that it makes public a private act, shines a light on one of the most hidden and complex language skills. Students can see writing unfold; they can get real insight into how to write an autobiography without making them "bed-to-bed stories," sequential stories that lack detail and flow (Hillocks 2007).

Modeling often means sharing a prewritten rough draft, either on an overhead or as a printed copy passed out to students. These drafts, which become sources of topics and inspiration for the Galway students, have included stories from several tutors about:

- pride in his Native American heritage
- how one teacher inspired her to become a teacher
- his days as a minor league ball player

- her husband and children
- how his school was just like Galway
- why she loves to write music

Teaching Organization and Argument Through Persuasive Writing

The autobiography unit is followed by one on persuasive writing, in which students must make and defend arguments on a specific topic. This writing is less self-centered than autobiography, requiring the Galway students to think more about the logic of their arguments and make them clear to their audience. It requires more audience and writer awareness.

On the first day of the unit during the year Megan participated in the project, a tutor gave a lesson on organizing arguments for why Galway High School should or should not be closed. This controversial topic hit home since the school had just announced it would be closing in May. The tutor, Rebecca, knew students would be passionate about their arguments. Rebecca wrote *Pros* and *Cons* on the board and asked students to volunteer answers for each. There was a catch, however; in order for Rebecca to accept an argument and write it on the board, the student had to provide a logical reason for the argument. For example, a student couldn't say, "Because it's not right." Rather, Rebecca challenged the student to think about why it isn't right to close the school. She asked, "Who is it not right for? How does it affect those people, and why is it bad?" By the end of the lesson, kids were noticeably fired up, and the board was full of pros and cons. When students couldn't come up with any more reasons, Rebecca divided the class into two; one side became proponents of closing the school, and the other side became opponents of closing the school. Rebecca asked each side to select their three best reasons and prioritize them. Within five minutes, Rebecca transformed an often lethargic class into an excited, competitive, and eager-to-prove-our-side-is-right group of students. Anywhere we turned, we saw students vigorously debating and defending their arguments. The room was noisy, but kids were working.

After ten minutes of letting sides make their decisions, Rebecca distributed a handout (see Figure 2.1) that helped the students outline their arguments and evidence in a clear, logical form. Each side then chose a representative to argue its case in front of the class, and judges were appointed to determine who made the best arguments. Like most high school students, the Galway students enjoy sociable games like these that give them the chance to express their opinions. Students from each side eagerly raised their hands, and the battle over the topic continued until the entire class agreed on the best argument. This lesson helped students see the importance of making logical, prioritized, and valid arguments. Students used similar handouts (scaffolding sheets) in all of their persuasive writing assignments.

Writing Prompts

After this introductory lesson, students were given a variety of writing prompts, such as the following one, to choose from and argue.

Team Extended Response Writing Prompt

Teenagers should not be allowed to drive until they are eighteen years old. At sixteen, they are too young and irresponsible. Driving is new to them, and they don't understand that being behind the wheel of a car is a serious thing. In 2002, more than five thousand teens ages sixteen to nineteen died of injuries caused by motor vehicle crashes (Centers for Disease Control and Prevention 2006). Teens are too busy talking to friends, listening to loud music, or talking on their cell phones to pay attention to the road.

If we can't raise the driving age, we should at least make it a law that teenagers aren't allowed to drive with other teenagers in the car unless there is an adult with them. With the excitement and hype of young people becoming independent drivers, we need to think about the safety of others along with the driver. A new law might decrease driving fatalities among young people. With lives on the line, we cannot afford to let irresponsible, inexperienced drivers behind the wheel of a vehicle.

Do you agree or disagree with the writer? Make an argument for or against the writer's statement using both evidence from the passage and your personal experience to support your answer.

Top Three Reasons Why the State Should Close or Not Close Galway High School

Argument 1:
Least strong argument (out of your top three)

_____

_____

Evidence (explain why)

_____

_____

_____

_____

_____

Argument 2:
Second strongest argument

_____

_____

Evidence (explain why)

_____

_____

_____

_____

_____

Argument 3:
Most powerful argument

_____

_____

Evidence (explain why)

_____

_____

_____

_____

_____

FIGURE 2.1 _Top Three Reasons Why the State Should Close or Not Close Galway High School_

In their persuasive writing lessons, tutors tried to match suggested topics with the interests and inclinations of the students. One tutor created this list of controversial topics that required students to do research to support their arguments.

1. Plastic surgery: Should people under eighteen years of age be allowed to have plastic surgery?
2. School uniforms: Should schools require students to wear uniforms?
3. Cloning: Should science pursue the cloning of a human being?
4. Lowering the drinking age: Is this a good idea?
5. MP3 file sharing: Is downloading material from the Internet without paying a fee fair or ethical?
6. Capital punishment: Should the government be allowed to put people to death?
7. Extending the school year: Would going to school all year increase the amount of learning?
8. TV violence: Does violence on TV make young people more violent?
9. High school athletes advancing to the NBA: Should there be a restriction on entering the NBA directly from high school?
10. A topic of your choice, after receiving teacher approval.

Working with our Galway students, we noticed many of them had trouble organizing their ideas on paper. Some students had several arguments in each paragraph, while others couldn't express an intelligible argument at all. Here was our chance to teach the kids a great writing strategy. We teachers can't assume students understand the writing process, even if they have been writing in the classroom for many years. Kylene Beers (2003) taught us that students need to be taught strategies and tips on how to become a better writer, and we needed to relearn this lesson. At Galway, tutors walked through the class, stopping at desks to help Galway students shape their writing, but we wanted the kids to do the work. Once their prewriting was complete, students were given the handout shown in Figure 2.2 to help them organize and articulate their arguments. This simple scaffold eliminated, for the most part, the need for a teacher to spend class time correcting an unorganized rough draft.

Hal's Worst Class Ever: The Project's Big Challenge

The "worst" class in the project came during the persuasion unit, which starts about the third week. (Remember, it takes about seven weeks for the tutors and the Galway students to establish permanent relationships.) This particular year there were over forty tutors covering a class of about twenty-five seniors—our first (and only) senior class.

Prewriting Outline
Persuasive Essay

I. Topic: Choose two of the topics from the provided topic list or a topic(s) of your own (with our approval). Write one or two sentences about why the topic is interesting to you.

Choice 1:

Topic: _____

Reason: _____

_____

_____

_____

Choice 2:

Topic: _____

Reason: _____

_____

_____

_____

II. Topic Decision: Critically evaluate the two topics you listed above. Choose the topic for which you will be able to build the best argument to persuade a reader to accept your side. Complete the statements below based on this decision. **(Hint: The statements below will help to build your introduction and thesis statement.)**

The statement that I can prove in my persuasive writing essay is:

_____

_____

I think this is the best choice for my persuasive writing topic because:

_____

_____

_____

continues

FIGURE 2.2 *Prewriting Outline: Persuasive Essay*

III. Points of Evidence: Based on your Internet research, list the three points of evidence that you found to support your argument. Give one or two sentences detailing what the source said about the point. **(Hint: The three points will become the body of the essay.)**

Point 1: _____

Details: _____

_____

_____

_____

Point 2: _____

Details: _____

_____

_____

_____

Point 3: _____

Details: _____

_____

_____

_____

IV. Conclusion Statement: Complete the statement below to summarize your argument. **(Hint: This statement will help to build the concluding paragraph.)**

Based on the three points of evidence, I conclude that:

_____

_____

_____

_____

_____

_____

FIGURE 2.2 *Continued*

The autobiography unit had gone fairly well, but I could tell that the Galway kids felt uncomfortable with all the hovering—the tutors seemed to be competing for high school students to interact with.

Galway has a small technology room funded by the university. Since the tutors responsible for the persuasive unit wanted to use these technology options during the unit, on the first day all sixty-five of us jammed into this small room.

The lesson was not bad; it used some provocative footage from the *American Idol* TV show, and the tutors led a discussion about the appropriateness of what we had just seen—a female singer who was a little overweight was ripped apart by the celebrity judges, who claimed she had the wrong body shape to be a star.

Several kids wanted to speak and raised their hands, but other students jumped in without raising their hands. One tutor, showing attitude, reprimanded the Galway kids who were "shouting out" their opinions yet ignored the raised hands. The atmosphere turned hostile, and the bell rang with the tutor explaining what the kids should have noticed.

The next project session, Sally grabbed me before I entered the room: "My Galway students are very angry, and I have separated our classes." She told me her students felt "dissed" by the college students. I told Sally that if it came to that, I was prepared to take my students back to the university and end the project. She said, "I never thought of that," but I could tell the idea was taking hold. "Why don't we discuss the issues with our classes, separately at first, and in twenty minutes you send a delegation of four tutors to my Galway class and I will send four high school students to you." So that is what we did.

I felt drained as I opened the discussion. The tutors started whining.

"These kids don't respect us."

"Kids in my high school would never act this way."

"Galway students are so rude; they don't listen to what we say."

I have never seen such a divisive and authoritarian way of looking at high school kids. I felt there was little hope of salvaging the project until one of our quiet young tutors, Joy, who was sitting in the back, raised her hand: "My kids are slowly opening to my group; I know they feel we are always around them and they need some space, but they have started to write and write on topic, with their hearts in it."

Other tutors murmured in agreement. "My kids are working and cooperating," Jon said.

"How can we save this?" Bethany asked.

At this point, the Galway students arrived. They also started by complaining.

"You treat us like we are kids and you are big teachers, which you are not."

"You are always on top of us; leave us alone to write."

"You don't listen; all you do is make rules and give orders."

Once again I thought there was no hope. I asked the Galway students if there was any way to save the project and make it possible for us to stay.

Suddenly everything changed. The Galway students' expressions softened, and one of them said, "We don't want you to leave. We like having you here. We just want you to respect us more."

One of the college students asked what more respect meant, and everyone began to discuss the project and its future. Sally said the same thing happened in her class. Her students really wanted us to stay, but to chill.

This was the first time I'd ever felt the project could collapse. However, the glue that bound us was so strong that these high school kids were not going to let us leave. They wanted us to change, and we needed to—and did. The project remained bumpy and difficult, but it never again approached collapse. We went on to experience a lot of fine writing, some great lessons, and one of the best showcase parties ever.

■ The Extended Response Unit: Teaching Students How to Write Under Pressure

Writing emails, memos, and reports and taking tests are just four tasks from the long list of routine writing people do in their jobs and daily lives. Every semester students complain that their future career won't require writing, and every semester we show them that no matter what field they pursue—doctor, policeman, teacher, nurse, lawyer, first responder, medical technician, office supervisor, electrician, carpenter—they will have to communicate through writing, and some of this writing will have to be completed quickly, without much time to rethink, revise, or edit. The extended response unit is designed to prepare students to write well under pressure and give them strategies for quickly formulating thoughtful responses during proficiency tests and any other timed writing (Gere, Christenbury, and Sassi 2005, 139). The writing assignments in this final unit incorporate all the skills they have learned throughout the project—prewriting, drafting, organizing, and now revising and publishing.

The following assignment is one of our favorites. Based on an idea in Frank McCourt's *Teacher Man* (2005), the prompt (see Figure 2.3) has very little structure, but it has a lot of imagination and led to one of the most memorable classes in the project, during which many Galway students read their excuses—a genre they had spent a lifetime perfecting—out loud to laughter and applause.

The tutor whose idea this was felt the students would relate well to the assignment, and was he ever right. But he also set up this lesson for success. He began by reading his own silly excuse note, and he kept it light. Students went after this topic as if they loved writing. And when the time came to read the excuses aloud—into a real, amplified microphone—the Galway alphas almost ran to the front of the room.

Make No Excuses

Pick one of these people to write about. Give an argument for what they did or did not do. Make yourself the parent or guardian for this person, and write me an excuse note for them. Please back up your argument with three points. The writing assignment must have three paragraphs that thoroughly explain your argument. This assignment must be turned in by the end of the period.

1. Make an excuse for anything about Michael Jackson.

2. Make an excuse for or against Adam and Eve.

3. Make an excuse for LeBron James.

4. Make an excuse for George W. Bush.

5. Make an excuse for Paula Abdul.

6. Make an excuse for Britney Spears.

7. Make an excuse for Ryan Seacrest.

8. Make an excuse for LL Cool J.

9. Make an excuse for Tupac.

10. Make an excuse for you.

FIGURE 2.3 *Make No Excuses*

Everyone applauded and cheered after readings that were filled with emotion, voice, and humor.

One of our quietest students, Tiffany, broke through with this lesson and allowed a tutor to read her work out loud. Tiffany made an excuse for Michael Jackson ("Is he white? Is he black?"), perhaps because, like Michael, she felt she did not quite fit in. (A former "cool" friend was pushing her away at the time.) Tiffany was proud of her work and delighted by the applause and cheering after the tutor read it in front of the class. From that day on, Tiffany became a hardworking and dedicated student.

We also gave the Galway students another simple prompt that seemed to work well for many.

- Part 1 (Plan A): Everyone has a dream job. Please create an extended response based on your dream job.
- Part 2 (Plan B): Sometimes, a person's dream job is just that—a dream. For a moment, imagine that your Plan A fell through and it is now up to you to think of a backup plan. Create an extended response on your fallback job.

This prompt worked because most of our students had thought about Plan A and really cared. Yet, reality strikes in Plan B. Since the topic was so personal, students thought about it and took it seriously. The writing was fresh and came from some genuine feelings and thoughts.

Extended response is the third and final writing unit, and the Galway students have come a long way since those first autobiographical pieces. They have had lots of practice using the writing process and are writing with more independence and confidence. Our evidence? Students may still be complaining about writing, but they are doing it. If the topic grabs them, many of them attack it immediately and show great interest in readers' reactions. They definitely write more, with more detail.

As a break from writing alone, which students have been doing for a long time now, we end this unit with the Writing Relay Game, a collaborative activity in which students share the writing. It is a fun way to write under pressure as a team and to practice the kind of writing skills students will need to take standardized tests and other exams. The tutors follow these steps.

1. Divide students into groups of four.
2. Give students a handout with a simple prompt.
3. Allow the first student in each group one minute to write on the handout and pass it on to the next student.
4. Give the next two students two minutes each to write and pass it on.
5. Give the last student five minutes to write.

Figure 2.4 shows an example of one result.

WRITING RELAY

DREAMS OF GLORY:

Imagine you have just won the lottery. How will you feel, and what will you do with the money? Do you see any conflicts that may arise?

Yes! I won the lottery. This is the best day of my life. I can't believe how lucky I am to have won the 53 million dollar jackpot. I wonder what I'll do with the money.

I feel so excited and overwhelmed. When I went to get my money I was smiling and smiling. The clerk put the money in my hand and I almost melted with happiness. I just stood there holding the money in hand looking dumbfounded. I got in my car and asked myself, "What am I going to do with all of this money?" and so many thoughts ran through my mind. I sat there and decided to put half in the bank and

FIGURE 2.4 *Writing Relay*

Every semester, tutors experiment with writing prompts, trying to think of new ones. Inevitably a few prompts will not work, usually because a tutor hasn't had enough time to build relationships with Galway students and is still unaware of their interests, lifestyle, and academic strengths and weaknesses.

For example, one time Tricia decided to build the song "Hands," by Jewel, into her extended response lesson. In the song, Jewel tells listeners that our world is innately good and that everyone has the power to help other people in need. "Hands" may be a well-written and beautiful song, but Jewel's words and message are far removed from the concerns of Galway students. Portia might have been speaking for the entire class when she asked, "Why didn't you pick a song by Tupac? His songs are poetic and we can relate to his words." When Tricia passed out her extended response handout that asked students to interpret the words of the song, a few students made an effort, but many of them wrote down meaningless answers. By the end, Tricia realized she could have had a productive lesson if she used her knowledge about her students to pick a song that connected with their lives. Interestingly, Tricia learned to love the urban school and its challenges and is well on her way to a career as a city high school English teacher. She recently and very successfully finished student teaching in a school very much like Galway.

■ Elements of Writing in Every Unit: Editing, Revision, and Publication

By the end of the extended response unit, Galway students are pretty much written out. They claim they have done more writing in this class than anywhere else, and an intensive writing program is indeed one of our goals. But quantity does not mean quality. So we do try to develop the program gradually. We have learned from scholars such as James Moffett (1987) and Jerome Bruner (2004) that writing assignments are best when they are progressive, going from simple autobiography to more complex persuasion and finally to extended critical responses. Each of our units has a purpose:

- autobiography: to help all of us find out about each other and to give our students a chance to express themselves about a subject they know best—themselves
- persuasion: to help students develop logical and powerful arguments about issues they care about
- extended response: to help students produce an immediate product

Unfortunately, standardized tests are fast becoming a way of student life. So the more experienced and comfortable students become with writing quickly about an assigned topic, the better they will do on these high-stakes tasks. Since the built-in time constrictions make extended response the most challenging unit, we present it after students have experienced autobiography and persuasion. But we also try hard to make this unit as relevant and interesting as possible, by carefully crafting lessons on topics that are meaningful and powerful.

Hal's Three-Day Lesson on Revision

The Galway students were willing to draft, and after they had bonded with their tutors, they often took an interest and even pride in what they wrote. But it was hard to teach these students to revise. Writing is one thing, but convincing high school students that they need to rewrite and make significant changes in their writing may be wishful thinking. Our tutors were able to convince students that they need to edit—make sure the punctuation, spelling, and grammar follow conventions—but to convince them to make big changes to improve their writing was a trip.

After students were seated and quiet, I introduced the lesson by asking for travel stories. "Tell the class stories you have had about bad travel experiences—but the stories cannot be about death or about getting upset stomachs." (Vomit stories are never fun.)

Galway students always have these stories—from cars that break down to brothers that temporarily disappear. The students get more and more involved after the bravest tell their tales of woe. Usually the stories are followed by groans and comments of sympathy, but all of the stories are about temporary, but daunting, travel problems. After twenty minutes of student stories, I told the students that I had written a rough draft of a travel story that I loved very much but that still needed to be revised.

This is the crux of the lesson (and the point that differs from what we learned about writing when we were in school): I am revising this piece because it is a compelling story. Students are conditioned to believe we change bad writing and make it good. The idea that to change writing is to admit the first attempt was a failure is deeply embedded.

My point is the exact opposite: a draft is a draft, filled with false starts, language experiments, colloquialisms, slang, informal grammar, and misspellings. However, inside a draft may be the seeds of a fine piece of writing. Thus, the only reason to change a draft is because it is so powerful that it is worth the effort. I believe this approach to writing changes the entire nature of how students look at drafting, revision, and editing. I may or may not get this message across, but I keep trying.

Here's my first draft, which every student received a copy of.

My Worst Flight

I do not love to fly, but I do anyway. My family and I were traveling abroad for the first time, to France for a visit with distant relatives. The first part of the flight left from Cleveland and was supposed to leave about 2 p.m. It was TWA. We got on the plane and were about to leave when we were told that thunderstorms would delay our flight to Kennedy airport, so we got off and waited for an hour in the terminal. We knew some people that were also on the flight, so we talked to them in the lobby. About 3 p.m. we got back on the plane and it took off. A lot of passengers were worried that they were going to miss connecting flights. Most people on the plane were going overseas because this plane was landing at the International Terminal at Kennedy. We were not worried because our flight to France wasn't scheduled to leave until about 11 p.m. that evening. We had plenty of time. The ride was kind of bumpy and our friends on the plane complained a lot about the delay, although the stewards and stewardesses fought back insisting it was the weather. When we arrived at the TWA terminal in New York, the weather was ominous, soon breaking into one of the worst thunderstorms I had ever seen. We went to the International Terminal where we planned to wait the six hours for our chartered flight on a small, unknown airline where comforts are short but seats are cheap. We got to the International Terminal by bus provided by the airport. On the way we passed the famous Saarinen-designed TWA terminal. I enjoyed looking at the different terminal buildings. When we got to the International Terminal we were the only ones there except for airline personnel. It was obviously a cheap airline because the terminal was poorly decorated, kind of barren and depressing. We were lucky in that we were able to check in this early, but we had not much to do until the plane was scheduled to leave at 11 p.m. We had packed our dinner, so we went to an empty bar-restaurant and ate our sandwiches, watching the activity of the airport from the big glass windows. After dinner we went back to the main area of the terminal where most people were arriving and it was filling up with lots of kids running around. I went to a candy shop in the terminal where the clerk advised me that the plane was going to be delayed for hours. I went back to my family despondent at the news. 11 p.m. came and went but by now the terminal was crowded with the people that were going to fill this 747. We soon heard a rumor that buses were going to take us to a Holiday Inn where we could spend the night, although the flight was now scheduled to leave about 6 a.m. The bus scene was awful. Too few buses for too many people. I was separated from my family who were taken first and then I was put on a crowded bus where I had to stand in a crowded aisle and wait on the hot bus. Finally I was taken to the Holiday Inn where I was reunited with my family and we tried to check in. Much to my dismay I discovered that the airline was not putting us up for the night at all. They were just giving us a banquet meal, a meal I absolutely did not want and could hardly eat. By now it was 2 a.m. My family and I found an empty conference room. My children and I slept on the floor while my wife wrote a letter. At 3:30 a.m. the buses arrived we were told by a screaming person who jarred the children and myself awake. My exhausted family and myself trudged to the buses that took forever to load. By 3:45 a.m. we were back at the terminal and in line to board the plane. The only problem was there seemed to be no plane. We waited for an hour and twenty minutes until this line moved. I was angry at this point and asked for my money back from an airline representative, who promised to look into it, but disappeared permanently. Finally, at 5:30 a.m. we were on the plane, a cramped 747, but we had a blanket and pillow nicely wrapped in plastic bags. We settled in and fell asleep as soon as the plane took off. Not quite 55 minutes into the flight I was awakened by this announcement. Because of flap problems, we have to turn around and go back to New York. I turned to my wife and remarked casually, "I don't think they can land the plane without flaps." My wife looked terror stricken. Basically the passengers around us were fairly calm. I asked a stewardess if it was going to be a rough landing and she said no. Fifty-five minutes later we landed smooth as silk at Kennedy where we were kept on the plane for about a half hour before we were allowed off. It was midmorning by now and I really wanted out of this flight. I went to the airlines agent screaming to refund my money. I wasn't the only one. A man quietly told the agent that he feared for the health of some of the elderly passengers. Meanwhile, people were passing around juice and cookies to the exhausted passengers sprawled out on the terminal floor. It was like a scene out of a disaster with Red Cross workers trying to help. I wanted to walk out of there and rent a car to drive home. But we stayed. By 10 a.m. a new airplane arrived and by 11 a.m. we were all boarded. My children slept for the entire flight. I slept through most of it, having nightmares about endless long lines that went nowhere. (Foster 2002, 195–97)

For the remainder of class that first day, we read the draft out loud, round-robin style. The next day, I told the students I wanted their help revising "My Worst Flight" and that we'd approach the revision in five steps (see Figure 2.5).

1. Create paragraphs and organize them in a logical order. (This is the simplest task.)
2. Cut parts of the story that don't fit or are unnecessary to the meaning. (This is still relatively easy to do.)
3. Add more details or information where the writing is vague. (This is the hardest thing to do.)
4. Examine word choices.
5. Anything and everything else.

I asked the students, in tutor-headed subgroups, to reexamine "My Worst Flight," notice that it is one big paragraph, use the scaffolding sheet as a guide to making as many revisions as they saw fit, and be ready to discuss their changes.

Tutors helped the Galway students revise "My Worst Flight" for about two-thirds of the period, and the students enjoyed having full authority to "attack" my writing. If

Help Me Make "My Worst Flight" as Good as It Can Be
Revising Ideas

Paragraphs

This story is one big, gloppy paragraph. Where should the paragraph breaks go? Place them with the proper marks in the text.

Why?

_____

_____

Cutting

It is always good to cut from a paper. First, figure out what you think the main or major points of this paper are. Write them here:

1. _____

2. _____

3. _____

4. _____

Cut whatever sentences, phrases, and/or sections you feel are not relevant to the main points. Go ahead, take your pencil and put lines through stuff. We'll discuss. Nothing is final until the author agrees (unless he gets really stubborn).

Why did you cut these parts?

_____

_____

More Information

Circle places where you feel the author could add more information or detail or story.

Explain to the author why this would help the work.

_____

_____

Write questions or comments to the author that would help him add some parts. Here is an example:

What happened on the bus ride to the hotel? What were the other people doing? Sleeping? Was anyone standing on the bus? Can you show how the bus was crowded?

_____

_____

continues

FIGURE 2.5 *Help Me Make "My Worst Flight" as Good as It Can Be: Revising Ideas*

Word Choices
Circle or change words or phrases that you feel can be made more interesting or more accurate.

What words or phrases did you select to change? Why? What do you recommend for the changes?

_____

_____

_____

_____

_____

Anything and Everything Else
What else can you offer this writer to help make this a great essay?

For instance:

1. Do you want to move some sections or sentences around?

_____

2. Where and why?

_____

_____

_____

3. What else?

_____

_____

_____

_____

_____

_____

Finally, pat the author on the back. Tell him he did a great job, and it is time to edit.

Let's look at all the punctuation, spelling, and grammar.

Then let's publish.

FIGURE 2.5 *Continued*

we teachers use our own writing as a model to be publicly revised, we demonstrate that revision is not an attack, but rather a method of changing an informal draft into a public, polished statement.

When the enthusiasm started to taper off, I brought the class back together and placed a transparency of "My Worst Flight" on the overhead projector. Then I asked for volunteers to come up to mark suggestions with an erasable marker. Ideas came from all corners of the room.

Students often contradicted one another, and arguments broke out. Some students wanted to cut where others wanted to add. Everyone agreed to cut the line, "We knew some people that were also on the flight, so we talked to them in the lobby."

"Not relevant," they exclaimed. And also, "Eliminate the line, 'Most people on the plane were going overseas because this plane was landing at the International Terminal at Kennedy.'"

Students asked me a few questions about things they thought required more information.

- "Why were you separated from your family?"
- "Who were your family members?"
- "Why did the candy counter clerk know about the flight?"

I didn't always agree with their suggestions, such as cutting the beginning sentence, "I do not love to fly, but I do it anyway." I liked that beginning, but if I've learned anything about writing, it's that editors and writers do not always agree, and I respected the reasons the students had for cutting the opening. It is a good lesson for all of us to remember that no matter how one approaches revision, it is tough for a writer to have someone else change his or her work.

Skills, Grammar, Editing, Minilessons

Galway students were required to edit at least one of their writing pieces into a formal draft. The class had a range of writers, but it had been bred into all of them that "correctness" was important. Perhaps this notion has become too ingrained in us all.

If young writers are concerned only with errors, then there is a good chance these novices will write little or nothing. They will not be focused on creating a story or describing an event; they will be concerned with correctness. How can we write if we are worried about getting it right the first time? Perhaps one of the big differences between an experienced writer and a beginner is the misperception that one must write perfectly, be "error free," the first time. This is one of the most serious blocks to effective writing. It is so important to allow students the freedom to write without fear of overzealous editing, at least in the initial stages of an assignment.

Editing is only one writing skill, and conventional wisdom to the contrary, it may not be the most important. The abilities to generate writing, to make arguments, to describe events, to be coherent, to structure and organize, to tell cogent stories, and to sequence are important writing skills too. Many aspects of the writing craft are more difficult and complex than editing. Of course, it's important to teach writers how to create writing that isn't distracting to readers, who expect the conventions of language to be intact. However, it takes so much more than comma placement or correct spelling to make writing work.

Some of the Galway students were able to edit with little help; others were never able to get it right even with help. The tutors were reluctant to overcriticize, particularly in the case of the fragile students who made the most errors.

Sometimes tutors edited for the students.

Sometimes tutors didn't edit enough.

Sometimes tutors were overbearing in their approach to editing.

Sometimes tutors got it right.

And sometimes having all those tutors hovering about made the Galway kids very nervous.

However, we tried to approach errors systematically. We classified mistakes based on how the errors impacted the meaning of the writing. For instance, all of our tutors were aware that errors could be classified into three broad types, ranging from type one errors, those that have the most negative impact on meaning, to type three, errors that have the least impact on the message of the writing (Foster and Newman 1988).

- *Type one: errors of clarity (syntactical errors).* Syntactical errors are the most serious because they can greatly interfere with meaning. These errors are exemplified by fragments, run-ons (although not all fragments and run-ons), and comma splices. Valerie Krishna (1975), referring to syntactical errors, writes:

> The [syntactical] error is a more serious, more fundamental mistake than the "classical" errors of verb agreement, punctuation, pronoun case, and so on that are systematically set out in the grammar books. A conscientious teacher will recognize the gravity of the problem and will wish to deal with it before moving on to work on conventional errors of detail.

  Donna M. Kagan (1980) is in agreement when she writes, "The sentence fragment and the run-on sentence are the most prevalent and irremediable errors found in grammatically deficient prose." These types of errors are seldom found in published writing. (We didn't find many of these types of errors. Most of our Galway students wrote with the meaning intact.)

- *Type two: errors of convention (mechanical errors).* These errors (e.g., subject/verb disagreement; comma, period, and question mark misuses; misspellings of common words) are the most common mistakes found in theme papers, and they can be serious when they interfere with comprehensibility. These errors often lead readers to dismiss the writer, ignoring the message and judging the messenger negatively.

- *Type three: errors of subtlety.* These are the least severe errors, and most writers make a few of them throughout their lives. They may include semicolon errors, quotation errors, citation errors, misspellings, and misuses of seldom-used words.

With these three types of errors in mind, our tutors attempted to consider the following editing guidelines.

1. Errors in written composition are not all equally serious.
2. The most serious errors are those that interfere with the message. These errors are mostly type one, sentence-level errors, such as fragments, fused sentences, and run-ons. Syntactical errors that severely disrupt meaning are very uncommon. Writing simple sentences and working on sentence practice may be one key to remediating these serious errors.
3. The least serious errors are those that hardly hinder the comprehensibility of the writing. These errors are usually subject/verb disagreement, misspellings, and common punctuation mistakes. These are very common errors, and they do tend to discredit the writer in the eyes of many readers.

4. Errors need to be remediated in order of seriousness, since most young writers can integrate only a limited amount of suggestions at a time.

5. Some errors are a result of risk taking. Often these involve semicolons or quotation marks.

We realize that the small errors are the ones that make so many readers so angry. Writers get marginalized and judged by these errors. Writers are so often ignored and the message lost in this kind of judgmental reading. Although a writer who makes these errors may be well organized, interesting, detailed, and persuasive, too many of these errors stop many readers in their tracks. These errors are the bane of our Galway students' existence. We keep trying, through minilessons, examples, peer reading, and direct grammar lessons, to get our students to see and change these errors, and certainly there were and are kids who write in formal English. But try as we might, we never completely get rid of these nasty, often speech-driven, pesky mistakes that many readers notice at the exclusion of all other skills. We all know that our Galway students will never be let into the "club" if they do not figure out the code. We hope we have planted at least a will to write and an understanding of the necessity of writing skills, so that someday our Galway students will figure out how to go that last step of learning: how to write without making people take notice of their "inadequacies." At any rate, we try.

Some of the informal usages are mistakes, misspelled words such as *where* for *were*, for example. But some of the informal language is simply a "grammatical echo," a term used by Rebecca Wheeler and Rachel Swords (2006) for "when the grammar patterns of a person's first language transfer into his or her expression in another language or language variety" (9). We try very hard to communicate the idea that language is relative, and that formal usage is appropriate in some settings and informal usage is appropriate in others. Unfortunately, not all readers are as kind as we try to be, and all of our students will benefit by knowing how to use formal language in certain settings such as the school world or business world.

In the real world of Galway students, editing boils down to two broad approaches. The first is working one on one, helping students understand, isolate, and correct. The second is teaching skill minilessons.

Minilessons: Skills for Developing Writers

Before students began their writing tasks each day, whoever was teaching gave short skill lessons. Thus the minilesson, as introduced to us by Nancie Atwell (1998), was a large part of our approach to improving skills and helping Galway students edit their work. Minilessons are short for several reasons.

1. The attention span of high school students is also short, particularly when it comes to skills.
2. Repetition is a key ingredient in effective training in language skills, and minilessons lend themselves to repetition.
3. Being "mini," they have to be simple and very direct, which is an excellent approach to skill lessons.
4. Short lessons do not dominate the class. Time remains for the far more important work of real reading and writing.

Tutors had a set of rules for the preparation and delivery of minilessons. Minilessons had to:

- be between five and ten minutes, maximum
- include student participation
- be usage-based, not rule-based
- include fun, practical examples
- show a strong application to writing
- be turned into a game if possible

Our stronger minilessons were student-centered, not teacher-centered, and taught at the point of student need, not in isolation. These types of minilessons are difficult to accomplish for teachers who were taught that grammar and writing skills can be tackled only through drills and exercises. The research on this subject cited by Constance Weaver (1996) and George Hillocks (1986) shows no support for the direct teaching of grammar in isolation. Stephen King writes in his book *On Writing* (2000) that "one either absorbs the grammatical principles of one's native language in conversation and in reading or one does not" (118–19). All of this doesn't mean we know how to teach Galway students how to use formal English. We don't, and Hal has certainly tried to figure it out (Foster and Newman 1988). No one has completely figured it out as far as we know. Teaching formal grammar remains one of the deep mysteries of the literacy classroom.

However, when working with writing, it is important for teachers to know their students' strengths and weaknesses and to work from there. Once the tutors became familiar with the Galway students' writing habits, they were able to pinpoint their needs. For instance, tutors kept complaining kids had no concept of using transitions in their writing. They felt that once students learned the purpose of transitions, they would use them in their writing. So the tutors of the persuasive writing unit created a minilesson on transitions that included a three-minute introduction on the different stylistic usages and examples and then an activity. Before class, they prepared a poster with six columns (see Figure 2.6), along with strips of paper that had examples of transitional words:

The tutors first talked about why transitions are important and how students could use them to make their writing clearer. Then they asked students to place the correct transitions under the proper purposes on the poster. Afterward, they gave students a handout with purposes and examples of transitions (see Figure 2.7).

Consequently,
As a result,
Likewise,
Accordingly,
In sum,
For example,
In fact,
Therefore,
On the other hand,
For this reason,

Connecting two sentences through similarity	Showing a cause-and-effect relationship	Contrasting two different ideas	Showing evidence	Emphasizing a point	Concluding

FIGURE 2.6 *Transitional Words Poster*

Purpose of Transition	Transitional Words
Connecting two sentences through similarity	*also, in the same way, likewise, similarly, in a similar manner, in comparison*
Contrasting two ideas or sentences	*on the other hand, oppositely, however, in spite of, nonetheless, nevertheless, in contrast, on the contrary, yet, still*
Showing steps, order, or sequence of events	*first, second, third, next, then, finally*
Showing a cause-and-effect relationship	*accordingly, for this reason, consequently, hence, so, since, due to, therefore, thus, as a result*
Specifying time	*after, afterward, at last, at first, to begin with, before, immediately, meanwhile, later, currently, during, now, recently, simultaneously, then, subsequently*
Specifying place or location of something or someone	*above, below, adjacent, next to, beyond, here, there, in front, in back, nearby*
Showing evidence	*thus, for example, namely, for instance, in particular, specifically, to illustrate, to demonstrate, in other words*
Giving additional evidence	*additionally, again, also, in addition, and, as well, besides, equally important, further, furthermore, moreover, then*
Emphasizing a point	*above all, even, indeed, in fact, of course, truly, to be sure, granted, no doubt*
Concluding	*finally, in brief, therefore, in the end, in the final analysis, in short, thus, in sum*

FIGURE 2.7 *Transitional Words and Purposes*

Next, tutors showed the class a transparency of the following piece of writing and asked for a volunteer to read it aloud, thus giving students a chance to hear what writing sounds like and looks like without transitions.

How to Kick a Soccer Ball

I learned how to kick a soccer ball when I was in kindergarten. I don't remember the coach who taught me, but it might have been my dad. As an adult who has given up the sport but not her love of the game, I hope to teach my little boy or girl how to kick a soccer ball someday. The steps of kicking a soccer ball are easy. Practice is the only way to kick the ball with precision and power. Place the soccer ball on the ground and stand a foot behind the ball. Decide which foot you will kick with. Place your kicking foot directly behind the ball and your other leg, which should be one foot to the side of your kicking foot, will give you balance. Your hips should be square with the ball—the ball will go in the direction of your hips so be careful not to turn your hips to the side when you kick. When you are ready to kick the ball, bring your kicking leg backward and strike the ball with the inner edge of your foot. Remember to use your balance leg and hips to direct the ball straight. When you master the skill of kicking the ball in a straight line, practice kicking the ball from different angles. A wall is a perfect kicking companion—it will automatically give you back your ball.

After the students read the soccer ball story, the tutors asked them whether they thought it was clear and whether they could make it more comprehensible for a reader who knows nothing about soccer: "What is easiest for you when you're learning a new skill? Steps? Lists? Can you offer any advice to this writer about how to make this story clearer?" Cherry said that numbered lists were helpful to her; Derrick said that the story was hard to follow because it lacked order. Tutors invited students to come up to the transparency and add transitions to make the soccer ball story better (see Figure 2.8). When students ran out of suggestions, a tutor asked another student to read the new and improved story. The class agreed the story sounded much better when transitions were used to organize the steps involved in kicking a soccer ball. Tutors encouraged students to begin using transitions in their own writing, and for the last ten minutes of the class, students wrote their own stories infused with transitions.

The Galway students became better writers based on minilessons covering skills such as those listed in Figure 2.9. Yet the battle for correctness is just that—a battle, and one that never stops and is never completely won. The tutors and students made compromises in many of their public pieces. The final pieces hung on the wall at the end-of-semester party were not perfect. Some were in excellent shape; others were as good as the teacher and tutors could get them. But the measure of student progress

How to Kick a Soccer Ball

I learned how to kick a soccer ball when I was in kindergarten. I don't remember the coach who taught me, but it might have been my dad. [Still,] As an adult who has given up the sport but not her love of the game, I hope to teach my little boy or girl how to kick a soccer ball someday. [At any rate,] The steps of kicking a soccer ball are easy. [First, or To begin with,] Practice is the only way to kick the ball with precision and power. [First, or To begin with,] Place the soccer ball on the ground and stand a foot behind the ball. [Also,] Decide which foot you will kick with. [Next] Place your kicking foot directly behind the ball and your other leg, which should be one foot to the side of your kicking foot, will give you balance. [Above all,] Your hips should be square with the ball— the ball will go in the direction of your hips so be careful not [to] turn your hips to the side when you kick. [Then,] When you are ready to kick the ball, bring your kicking leg backward and strike the ball with the inner edge of your foot. [Most importantly,] Remember to use your balance leg and hips to direct the ball straight. When you master the skill of kicking the ball in a straight line, practice kicking the ball from different angles. [Infact,] A wall is a perfect kicking companion—it will automatically give you back your ball.

FIGURE 2.8 *How to Kick a Soccer Ball (with Revisions)*

was improvement, not perfection. Writing is not only about the product, it's also about the process. Although there was no formal scale, the high school students' portfolios told the story in the quantity and quality of writing and in the obvious growth that most of these students showed from the beginning of the semester to the end.

Hal on Train Wrecks: The Class That Ended Early

Every tutor prepared minilessons, but one semester we came up short, both in number and duration. First, we didn't teach the kids enough skills for their writing to improve. Second, our lessons were ending too early. Too many classes had ten or so minutes at the end during which the kids had nothing to do except hang out and wait for the bell . . . and every experienced teacher knows this is trouble.

Minilesson Topics

Grammar:

1. Transitions

2. Subject/verb agreement

3. Misplaced modifiers

4. Commas

5. Prepositions

6. Contractions

7. Independent clauses

8. Dependent clauses

9. Sentence fragments

10. Run-on sentences

11. Quotations marks

12. Vocabulary—what every writer needs to know

Writing:

1. Differences between formal and informal writing

2. The writing process

3. Essays

4. Sentence structure

5. Research—books, journals, articles

6. Internet research

7. Proper citation

8. Plagiarism

9. Getting started

10. Brainstorming

11. Paragraphing

12. Rough drafts

13. Final drafts and portfolio maintenance

FIGURE 2.9 *Minilesson Topics*

There is one episode in particular, between James and Alisha, that Megan and I refer to as "the train wreck." When the lesson ended early that fateful day, the Galway students started socializing. Alisha was sitting in the back near where Megan and I were standing. James walked toward Alisha and started an inappropriate and very suggestive dance at Alisha's desk. At that exact moment, the school district's curriculum director entered the room to set up for a meeting, saw what James was doing, and began screaming at him. James took her ranting for a few minutes but then mumbled a few choice words under his breath.

This turned into a back-and-forth cussing contest.

Megan kept looking at me with this pathetic expression that said in no uncertain terms, *You're the boss. Do something.* After an eternity, the bell finally rang and James and Alisha left. Megan and I left, too, thankful things hadn't deteriorated any further.

But there should have been a minilesson.

Dealing with Language and Race Issues

There is no denying that kids have a language of their own. Since they were predominantly African American, Galway students spoke to one another socially in African American language (Smitherman 2006, 9–12). However, in the classroom, despite the occasional vernacular expression to make a point or create humor, the Galway students were very capable of code-switching. They spoke to their black friends one way, to their teachers and tutors in a more formal way. It would be wrong to tell these kids to stop speaking their dialect and to use only formal English. What we can do is teach kids that language is variable, that different languages are appropriate in different situations. What all kids in every school need to know is how to code-switch—when, where, and how to use formal and informal language.

At Galway, tutors never felt, communicated, or in any way believed that African American language was inferior, as Keith Gilyard (1991) so often fears happens in schools. Geneva Smitherman (2004) points out to all of us that African American language "is not just the language of Black children and youth in the public schools, but also the language of the Black Church, of everyday folk, of seniors, of the working class, of preachers, of Nobel and Pulitzer Prize winners" (194). Kids need to know it isn't a matter of inferior versus superior language but rather of adapting or shifting our language to the setting, audience, and purpose. We conveyed to all involved in the project Smitherman's position that "African American Language (AAL), like all languages, is a tool for ordering the chaos of human experiences. AAL gives shape, coherence, and explanation to the conditions of U.S. slave descendants and functions as a mechanism for teaching and learning about life and the world" (2006, 64).

In discussions with my university classes, the linguist and Ebonics expert Arthur Palacas stated that most African Americans code-switch already. To enhance the ability to code-switch, Palacas (2006) recommends that teachers talk openly about language in the classroom:

> By showing respect for language—for the childhood language, for the mother tongue, for the language used with relatives and friends—by showing that respect, students become very open to the discussion of language. It's not a threat anymore; the threat has always been the threat to identity.

Palacas (2001) also insists that Ebonics is intellectually appropriate. He tells his African American students, "You grew up intellectually fine, no matter what people have thought about your language and your intellect that have caused you to sit in the back seat and not talk. It's all been false." Palacas asserts, "The school itself needs . . . a language policy that starts respecting language difference," and contends that the African American language is actually a language and not a dialect, a distinction that Smitherman (2004) feels is important because "in the minds of the lay public, languages have high status, dialects do not" (192).

Rebecca Wheeler and Rachel Swords (2006) posit there is a real problem with the terms *standard* and *nonstandard*. They point out that all languages or dialects are linguistically equal, but they differ in social status (13). But *nonstandard* implies inferior. So they argue for the use of *formal* and *informal*. "In our experience, the terms *formal* and *informal* are intuitively accessible. They capture the simple and uncontroversial notion that we all vary how we present ourselves setting by setting. Both adults and children understand these terms" (23). In our project, we consistently use *formal* and *informal* to define language, and we emphasize the need to use different languages in different settings. That has always been our position and viewpoint.

Our Galway tutors, most of whom had taken Palacas' linguistics course, approached language differences with all the above in mind, and no one witnessed an incident or uncomfortable moment that occurred because of differences in language use.

Although vernacular English, both black and white, was used and respected in the classroom in writing and speaking, the project did require at least one and usually several writing pieces to be revised and edited into formal English. Wheeler and Swords (2006) see this as transferring rather than as making mistakes. "If the children were not making mistakes in Standard English but instead were transferring in the detailed grammar patterns of their home language, then a whole different approach opened up. . . . [She] saw her way clear to recognizing and respecting the language of the home while adding the language of the school to her students' linguistic toolboxes" (11). This meant that students were required to edit out much of the vernacular as well as change misspellings and faulty grammar usage. After all, some language issues transcend dialect differences. Sometimes a mistake is a mistake.

Work Portfolios

Throughout the project, our teachers have always asked Galway students to maintain what we called, work portfolios. Galway students are given portfolios in which they keep all the work they do for the class. Each portfolio includes a simple recordkeeping sheet listing the date and the assignment. Although this seems simple enough and should work without flaws, it has been a thorn in our side from the beginning. We now predict that something will go wrong with the portfolio system each semester, but we never know what that something will be. The most common problem, of course, is missing portfolios. We now tally the portfolios before and after each class. The tutors color code the portfolios based on writing groups, but still something always happens, and by the end of the semester somebody's portfolio is missing.

Portia was a wonderful young woman who loved to play pranks and complain but had a personality and character that we came to admire deeply. It took a while to figure her out because she never stopped whining. Portia gave all of our tutors fits during the Shakespeare unit. We thought she was going to walk out, but instead she gave her all (although she complained about "the low performance level of her peers"). After pushing us close to a nervous breakdown, Portia was overheard to say that the Shakespeare unit had been fun.

Well. Even though we tallied all the portfolios and thought we knew where they were, when it came time to move into the second portfolio phase, the work portfolio, surprise, surprise, Portia's portfolio with all of her writing was missing. Through a complicated process we are incapable of describing, she figured out (after much stress on our part, of course, not on hers) that it was in the car of one of her friends, which was parked somewhere across the street from the high school. Hal walked her to the car as she, as usual, chatted the entire way, which was a substantial distance. When she and Hal got to the car, there was the portfolio, safe and sound.

But the worst thing ever to happen to the portfolios was fairly amazing. That semester, our tutors had it all figured out—all the portfolios were accounted for at all times. Unbeknownst to Sally or Hal, one of the tutors took all the portfolios home overnight to do some recordkeeping. While the portfolios were in his car, his car was stolen. Hal will never forget the stricken look on the tutor's face when he confessed what had happened. Hal was stricken too—how could this happen? But it did.

About a week later, the police found the car, stripped of course, but with the portfolios untouched in the backseat.

Years of these portfolio glitches have taught us to adopt certain procedures for portfolio maintenance.

- Set up "portfolio groups" of four or five students, which remain constant for all group work throughout the semester.
- Keep all portfolios alphabetized and in color-coded boxes according to group.
- Assign a tutor or a responsible student from each group to be in charge of maintaining his or her group's portfolio box; every portfolio should be in alphabetical order and in the correct group box by the end of class.
- Designate a teacher or tutor to verify that every student has her or his portfolio in the correct box and order. A student roster divided alphabetically by groups is effective for accomplishing this task.
- Never allow a student portfolio to leave the classroom. All portfolios must be accounted for before students can be released for the day.

Showcase Portfolios

Along with requiring that students maintain work portfolios, our writing curriculum also requires them to select one or two pieces of writing from the semester for a showcase portfolio to display at our end-of-semester party. Each of these showcase portfolios:

- is personalized by the student with cover designs such as drawings or pictures
- contains at least one writing piece selected for full revision and editing, which is shared with the class at the showcase party
- includes at least one or two additional writing drafts to show the writer's growth
- includes a reflection section (as shown in Figure 2.10)
- includes a personal, handwritten note from each tutor thanking the student for the experience and expressing a personal message about the public writing piece

Before starting our last unit of the semester, on Shakespeare, we devote an entire week of class time to helping Galway students select pieces, revise and edit their shared writings with their tutors' help, prepare their showcase portfolios, and write their reflections. At the end of the week, the portfolios are checked for completion and collected.

The showcase portfolio is one of the project's major instructional tools. It brings a tangible and undeniable closure to the writing. The progress of each Galway student is there for everyone to see. The formal piece is evidence of the ability to shape and control a composition from a draft to a revised and edited final version. These pieces are

Showcase Portfolio Criteria

Tutor will help you to prepare a showcase portfolio as outlined below.

- Select writing pieces to be included in your showcase portfolio. (Three of the following four pieces are required.)
    1. your featured (best written) piece for public display
    2. your favorite piece
    3. your most improved piece
    4. rough draft of your most improved piece

- Edit and type a final copy of your featured piece for public display.

- Type the showcase reflection summary. See "Questions for Showcase Reflection."

- Create your own artistic cover page for the portfolio. The cover should be about you, reflecting your interests and personality. The cover page should be titled:

Showcase Portfolio

of

Your Name

Date

- Organize the showcase portfolio in a folder.
    - cover page
    - blank sheet for featured piece/photos
    - showcase reflection summary
    - student's favorite piece
    - student's most improved piece
    - rough draft of most improved piece

continues

FIGURE 2.10 *Showcase Portfolio Criteria and Reflection Questions*

Questions for Showcase Reflection

Instructions:

Compose a rough-draft summary about your writing and composition pieces using the following four questions.

Revise and edit for clarity, mechanics, and correctness.

Type a final copy for inclusion in your showcase portfolio.

1. Why did you select this piece for public display? (Was it your favorite piece or your most improved piece?) Please explain.

   _____

   _____

   _____

   _____

2. What did you learn about yourself as a writer?

   _____

   _____

   _____

   _____

3. What do you need to do to be a better writer?

   _____

   _____

   _____

   _____

4. How will you learn to be a better writer?

   _____

   _____

   _____

   _____

FIGURE 2.10 *Continued*

taped to the wall, and during the end-of-semester party, readers, teachers, and Galway students offer responses on sticky notes that are then collected and also placed in the student portfolios.

Although there is always a mix of writers from remedial to proficient, all the Galway students show growth in their ability to write and at least make an effort at shaping the writing. But none of the tutors or Sally can do Hogwarts magic and turn some of the most challenged students into college-bound writers ready to compete with the wealthiest and most academically capable kids in the suburban and private schools.

The project isn't going to achieve that.

But it has achieved something else. Many of the Galway students write more than they have ever written before, try their hands at some sort of revising, and take pride—often for the first time—in a piece of writing that has been read and appreciated by a wide range of readers, including special guests such as professors, a principal, college department chairs, a dean, and others.

Portia told us:

> I know I'm a better writer because now when we're in class and the teacher tells us to write something or gives us a composition, we know from first-hand that we have to prewrite. She doesn't have to tell us that. We know that we have to brainstorm. We know that we have to use transitions. We know how to write beginnings, middles, and ends. We know what makes a letter, what makes a story; how we're supposed to do it. We know how it's supposed to be done. (Bahl 2006)

The Showcase Party

There is a huge difference between telling kids, particularly those with low self-efficacy, what they could become and telling them what they did become. At the end of every semester, we invite the high school kids to celebrate their achievements with the tutors, teachers, principals, and staff. The party is all about telling them what they did become, and it is an emotionally satisfying close to the project. We believe every class needs this type of experience, a shared culmination of the work and efforts over the course of a semester or even a year.

At the party, we celebrate in many ways.

- We eat, sometimes pizza, sometimes sandwiches, always cake and soda. (Free food is a big deal for many of these kids. We were reminded of the harsh reality of Galway at one of our parties when Colbee asked for more pizza to take home to feed her brothers.)
- We give out bags of candy, party favors, pencils, magnets, key chains.

- We give speeches. Representatives from each group talk—the high school kids, the college tutors, Hal, and Sally.
- A role model from the community gives a motivational and congratulatory speech to the students. Role models have included deans from a local college, foundation representatives, business leaders, and college administrators.
- We share the revised, ready-for-an-audience pieces of writing by posting them on the wall and encouraging sticky-note comments from the readers, comments that are positive, friendly, and loving.
- We give awards for the Shakespeare performance, sometimes certificates, sometimes candy bars.
- We ceremoniously give each Galway student his or her completed and attractively decorated showcase portfolio with personal letters from the tutors. This is usually followed by hugs, tears, and finally the recognition that a group of strangers who became friends through months of learning and teaching will become strangers again.

These kids have written and stretched themselves. Maybe they have not turned into contributors to the *New Yorker*, but they have seen the possibilities. And they have read Shakespeare, most with enthusiasm along with understanding. "What can't you read now?" we ask them.

Every class can have a celebration at the end of the semester or year. It doesn't take much, and it is so important to display the final products of the work students do. As long as it includes some kind of final portfolio of student work that is refined for public display, the ceremonial closing of an educational experience sheds much light on students' accomplishments. We highly recommend that teachers, particularly in urban schools where kids are so seldom celebrated, end their semester or year with the kind of experience we have just described. We know that our students leave the party with a spirit of hope and a sense that it is good for teachers to have high expectations and that they can meet those expectations. Our Galway students have been challenged academically and have found that they are up to it, maybe for the first time. The party allows us to show our gratitude to them and the pride we have in them. We all leave the party feeling that something unique and special has ended and we—tutors, teachers, students—sense the possibilities of the future.

Another Hal Story: You Can't Judge a Kid Until You Really Get to Know Him

Galway had gangs, so teachers and administrators tried to control behavior that seemed gang related. Certain colors were frowned upon if not banned, and once we had to retake group pictures because a couple of young men seemed to be making gang signs with their hands. In the one twelfth-grade class we worked with were two young men who had a strange rapport evidenced by a lot of private conversations and inappropriate laughter. On a day Sally was absent, I inadvertently placed them in the same group. She immediately separated them the next day, but they were forever communicating with what appeared to be gang signs. The alpha of the two, DeShawn, big and scary, always seemed a little aloof, although he cooperated on his own terms. He did his work but always seemed to be judging and looking for the angles. None of the tutors, nor Sally, nor me could have a heartfelt, honest conversation with DeShawn. He had no enthusiasm for writing, but he did it, articulately and quite well.

But he really got into the Shakespeare unit. He decided he wanted to play Hermia, the young woman who ran away with her lover, who her father despised. A born leader, DeShawn took over. He directed the rehearsals, kept his group on task, and put his entire personality into the performance of his scene.

The day of the performance, DeShawn wore a dress, spoke in a falsetto, and had memorized his lines, which was not required. Everyone else read the lines, albeit fluently and with deep understanding. DeShawn brought the play to a stop. He was so good that his peers gave him a standing ovation.

During a scene change, Sally asked me who the guy with the camera was. I'd noticed him too, a middle-aged, balding white man snapping pictures, and had assumed Sally had asked a friend to take some shots to document the occasion. We had no idea who he was. After the play, we asked him why he'd come to the performance. We were stunned to learn that he was DeShawn's agent! DeShawn was a media producer who had a brilliant way with computers and other technologies and was on the brink of a breakthrough as a recorder and developer of rap music.

We had pizza that afternoon, and DeShawn and I got our slices at the same time. I told him how effective he was as Hermia and how proud I was of him. He had tears in his eyes. We shook hands and sat down and ate.

I never saw DeShawn again, but Sally told me he didn't graduate because he couldn't pass the required math test. Who knows what happened to him. Nevertheless, I learned a valuable lesson about stereotyping and making judgments. I hope DeShawn is by now a successful producer.

Our Most Memorable Party

Our tutors are warned to be flexible. It is one of the most important qualities a teacher needs because something always happens. One semester *that something* happened at the party. We always hold the Shakespeare performance on the next-to-last day of instruction, the party on the last day. We need every bit of time we have to present the curriculum, prepare for the Shakespeare performance, and wrap things up with the party. There's no wiggle room. At the end of this particular semester, however, another teacher planned a field trip on our Shakespeare day; at least four of our students wouldn't be in class. So we decided to get our students released from their prior class on the final day of the semester and have both the performance and the party then. It was risky, but we had no choice.

Multiple scenarios have to collide to create a really awesome disaster, and they did. The administration did a hall sweep right before our play began, and at least six of our students were found in the hall without passes and sent to in-school suspension. They couldn't perform their roles in the play and were not permitted to come to the party. The tutors and other students filled in, but it was a loss for everyone, especially the kids who worked so hard and had to miss the payoff.

Sally always speaks at the party. This time she read a note that a student messenger had just delivered from one of the missing students, Tess, a young lady who was one of our most difficult students but who had gradually won our hearts. Tess wanted so badly to perform in our play and had written a wonderful persuasive essay about dialect, which was displayed on our wall for all to read. She'd come a long way, from a very reluctant writer to one who took pride in her work and was willing to put real effort into it. Here is part of what she wrote quickly that morning in in-school suspension:

> I would personally like to thank you for all you done. Without you guys I would never open up so much about my writing. You have help me accomplish a lot since you've been there. Thank you for sharing your experience with me. Thank you for dealing with me on my worst days, and my goofy days. Thanks for acknowledge my ideas and dream, for never giving up me even when i gave up on my self. You guys really have a gift, and I hope you continue to help kids, to achieve more and continue with their dreams. I will also remember you all. You all are forever in my heart and mind. When i feel as if I am going to give up, i will think of you all and try harder. Remember it only takes a child to tell you, you are encouraging; and that should be enough for you all continue your journey.
>
> With love and respect
>
> Tess

Some of you may view this paragraph as a disaster. What possible good did we do if that is how a student writes at the end of the semester? But we knew better. We knew that Tess was challenged from the beginning; that by simply rereading this out loud, she would solve the problems of the missing words and endings; that with some encouragement we could get Tess to explain why she felt this way and give detailed examples. We knew that this was one of her first attempts to write from her heart, a beginning that had taken twelve weeks to achieve. We also knew that she needed a fine teacher during her senior year who would nurture her further and move her another step toward a literate future. And we knew that no teacher has the magic to bring Tess in a single year where she needed to be to go to college or to train for any career that requires reading and writing. Tess was educable but way behind and at risk in the deepest sense. We left Tess a better reader and writer than we found her, but she had a long way to go. Although we were willing to help her continue her growth, we wouldn't have the opportunity and would most likely never find out what happened to her next.

After Sally read Tess' letter, there was silence. We were very moved, but there were no tears; the party ended with subdued farewells. Our tradition is to end by handing back the showcase portfolios that we collected the week before. We did just that, and the high school students silently sat reading their personal letters from Sally and their tutors. Everyone hugged, and the bell rang. The year was over.

Hal and one of the tutors decided to find Tess. The in-school suspension room was well hidden, and the monitor looked none too happy to have visitors. When Tess saw her tutor, she sprang from her desk, and they exchanged a loving, friendly embrace. The tears finally came, with the realization that something very special had come to an end.

What We Learned

- Create a "building curriculum." Start your writing workshop with a confidence-building writing assignment, such as autobiography, and examine student skill levels. From there, make the units progressively more challenging for students by honing in on writing skills, grammar, and vocabulary.
- Develop writing assignments that are based on student interests.
- Constantly reflect on the units to improve lessons and adapt them to student needs.
- Demonstrate brainstorming, writing a rough draft, revising, editing, and creating a final draft.
- Model for kids that the process of writing requires mistakes.
- Give students opportunities to write without fear of red ink.
- Present minilessons that are based on students' needs.
- Have minilessons and writing prompts ready every day in case lessons end early.
- Have open discussions with classes about languages—informal and formal, the purposes of different kinds of speech and dialects.
- Use portfolios to show and celebrate student writing.
- Have an end-of-semester celebration of student work.

3 Connecting Urban Students to Books

Inventing and Reinventing the Reading Workshop

■ Helping Students Choose to Become Readers

Galway High School was notorious for the lowest proficiency scores in the school district. In one of the attempts to improve the school's reading scores, the principal required that everyone in the building take part in a half-hour of silent sustained reading every Wednesday, during which time a student or a teacher sat reading in a rocking chair in a glass-enclosed display case. A clever gimmick, perhaps, but not enough to raise reading comprehension scores in a tough reading environment like Galway, where many of the kids did not read and most of them didn't like to read.

Four years ago, the principal of Galway asked Sally to include lessons to improve reading comprehension. So the project curriculum was adjusted to incorporate a reading workshop unit that included reading comprehension minilessons. This unit incorporated the following core principles.

- Read engaging materials in the classroom to improve reading ability (Allington 2001).
- Find books that connect to student experiences (Lesesne 2003).
- Build a classroom library of books for students.
- Take students to the school library.
- Empower students by allowing them choice in the books they read (Daniels 2002).
- Empower students by allowing open, personal responses (Probst 2004).
- Teach reading strategies that improve comprehension (Beers 2003).

- Teach minilessons on reading comprehension strategies before or after students read (Atwell 1998).
- Give students an opportunity to read for twenty or thirty minutes at least once a week (Allington 2001).

Many of these principles are based on the work of Richard Allington, Harvey Daniels, Kylene Beers, Teri Lesesne, Nancie Atwell, and Robert Probst.

- Allington (2001) shows how research supports the idea of reading workshops and sustained silent reading.
- Atwell (1998) teaches us how to create and manage writing workshops.
- Daniels (2002) helps us shape our literature circles and workshops with practical suggestions and teaching ideas that reinforce our basic values.
- Beers (2003) shapes reading strategies that help students comprehend books. We use her strategies throughout our minilessons.
- Lesesne (2003) shows us how to match books with students.
- Probst (2004) teaches us how to give voices to our students, empowering them to use their experiences to connect with the books they read.

Building reading workshops into our curriculum is our attempt to give students the opportunity to read books that connect directly with their life experiences. Our aim is to have students experience authentic and powerful reading as part of a comprehensive, meaning-centered curriculum. The reading workshops mesh tightly with our guiding themes.

Reading workshops have somehow come to be associated with elementary and middle schools. How can we claim reading workshops belong in a rigorous advanced curriculum? We strongly support the idea of some in-class reading in all classrooms. An International Baccalaureate student from another high school once told Hal that she wished her English class did some in-class reading because most of her peers didn't read the assigned books. These advanced kids had many strategies to bluff a teacher. At least if the beginning or some other part of a book has been read in class, the teacher has a little more knowledge and control. Also, Daniels points out that advanced students have the advantage of self-selecting rich and interesting books (2002, 227). That is exactly what we want to happen: to infiltrate interesting, complex books into the classroom.

Our first reading workshop was a baby step, on Fridays only, eight Fridays to accomplish everything that had to be done—introducing the books, matching students with the books, getting started, reading, presenting minilessons, and wrapping it all up. Needless to say, few students finished their books. However, we saw the workshop's potential—all of our Galway students, tutors, and teachers read. And many of the students enjoyed what they read even if they didn't complete the books.

The tutors felt that the Fridays-only approach did not work for a few reasons.

- Fridays were often disrupted by assemblies or pep rallies.
- Reading once a week was fragmented; it was difficult to maintain continuity.
- There was not enough time to finish the workshop.

Now we allot two continuous weeks to the workshop. Every semester, based on what we learn, we make changes, and we are sure additional changes will take place. But we are committed to giving our students a chance to read meaningful contemporary literature they have some voice in selecting.

Selecting Books

Whenever Sally is asked what makes a good urban teacher, she answers, "Relationships with students." Sally gets to know her students, really know them. She checks their files, talks to parents and guardians, and chats with her students during class-time lulls. Her students say Sally makes time for them and cares about them. She can be tough and demanding, but she is always loving and approachable. And she always tries to match what she knows about her students with the reading and writing choices she will inevitably give them.

So as we developed our reading workshop, we were not surprised that Sally requested we choose books that connected to her students' lives, primarily the African

American experience. As Alfred Tatum (2005) points out, "Young adults appreciate interesting reading material that makes sense to them. Texts should reflect reality, but they should also point the way to a different and better reality" (75).

The first big challenge was to find books that were acceptable in classrooms, without profanity or objectionable scenes. We soon gave up "acceptable" as a criterion because it is impossible to find sanitized relevant books. So we took our chances. We offered Galway students an array of choices, from *The Pact* (which Tatum recommends in particular for African American males) to *The Color of Water* to *I Know Why the Caged Bird Sings* to *A Raisin in the Sun* to *Hope in the Unseen* to *The Joy Luck Club*.

One semester we offered Galway students freedom to select their own books with our approval. Our guidelines included:

- strong, dynamic themes, such as overcoming adversity (*The Pact*) and dealing with complex racial issues (*A Raisin in the Sun*)
- multifaceted and interesting characters, such as the mother and her son in *The Color of Water*
- high literary quality, such as that of *I Know Why the Caged Bird Sings*

We hoped students would select books that were included in talks given by tutors and the librarian, books such as *Tears of a Tiger*, by Sharon Draper, and *The First Part Last*, by Angela Johnson.

We kept changing our approach because, although students truly did read in workshop, we were never certain how to connect the right books with the right students. Teri Lesesne (2007) states that reading level and length aren't important; making connections is. Alfred Tatum (2007) writes, "Like all adolescents, African American . . . adolescents want to know why they are reading the assigned materials and the benefits of reading the materials. They would like to know how the texts will enable them to be, do, think, or act differently as a result of reading them" (82). Thus, we were always looking for and finding books that reflected the modern African American experience.

To investigate whether giving students more freedom over book choice or presenting them with preselected books worked better, we decided to preselect five books for our students the following semester.

Megan's Secret for Turning Nonreaders into Readers

A group of four tutors headed the reading workshop, but Hal and I chose the reading selections beforehand. We met at a local bookstore to search for books that were culturally diverse, challenging to read, interesting, and—most important—able to reach our student readers. We wanted to offer students a choice, make different kinds of books available, all of them challenging and unique in their own ways. After an hour of scouring the shelves, we had five:

- *A Raisin in the Sun*, by Lorraine Hansberry
- *The Color of Water*, by James McBride
- *I Know Why the Caged Bird Sings*, by Maya Angelou
- *The Pact*, by Sampson Davis, George Jenkins, Rameck Hunt, and Lisa Frazier Page
- *Escape from Slavery*, by Francis Bok

We thought we had included a little something for every kind of reader—a play, two very different autobiographies, a novel, and a nonfiction adventure—about varying African American experiences. All five of these books pushed the reading level of our kids at Galway, but we knew these books had the potential to make their reading worthwhile and relatable.

Helping Hal choose books for Galway students made me think of my own journey as a reader. In high school, I was one of those kids whom all teachers worry about—I read books by way of SparkNotes, CliffsNotes, and the Internet. I'm not proud of that, but reading books, whether for school or enjoyment, gave me a headache. Classics like *All Quiet on the Western Front*, *The Good Earth*, and *Pride and Prejudice* did not interest me in the least, so instead of opening the real books, I found other ways to "read" them.

Maybe it was my lack of freedom of choice or boredom with books that were pushed on me that made me dislike reading . . . or maybe I didn't know interesting books existed. It wasn't until my English courses in college that I found an appreciation for reading, when I was able to choose what kinds of literature courses to take. I got involved in absorbing literature discussions that connected the books I read to my life, and I was hooked.

So choice must have something to do with becoming a reader.

I vowed to myself that when I encountered a student who refused to read or couldn't find an enjoyable book, I would remember what it was like for me as a reader in high school. My own education has taught me that if I want my students to read, I need to give them a proper balance of:

- freedom of choice
- books that connect to their lives
- books that challenge their reading level

I also realized the importance of getting students actively involved in and excited about what they are reading.

Collecting Books for the Classroom

Often, teachers are limited to the literature available in their school libraries or book rooms. "How are you going to pay for these books so that every student has the book he or she wants?" Sally asked us one day before we started the unit. We thought it wouldn't be too much to ask each tutor to buy one book, read it, and pass it on to a Galway student. One semester we had a small grant from the university, which included $500 for reading workshop books. This grant allowed us to buy six copies of six different books. Most of the time we did what any teacher would do, which is depend on the books in the library. With the cooperation of the librarian, we selected the most relevant books and made them available to our Galway students.

Sally is always on the lookout for books she can use in her classroom; she views each of her anthologies as a library collection placed inside one very heavy book. Harvey Daniels (2002, 92–93) discusses how teachers collect books for the classroom. Sadly he admits that teachers are nickel-and-dimed, "part-time scavengers, prowling garage sales" (93). Teachers often end up building their classroom libraries using their own money. This is a sad and tangible reflection of the inadequacies of our school system.

Selling Books to Students

According to Teri Lesesne (2007), "It's all in how you sell the book." Lesesne highly recommends a personal introduction to the books you suggest. We did just that. Tutors came to class on Friday with the books read and four-part presentations prepared to entice kids with the characters and plots. They promoted the books as if they were selling cars. Here is an example of a book talk for *Tears of a Tiger*.

1. Give hooks to get kids motivated to read the book.
    - "Remember those three students from Cartona High School who were killed by driving over a cliff?"
    - "Remember that teenage couple killed on the way to the prom last year? Their funerals were covered for two days in the local paper. Drinking and driving. It is the nightmare of every parent."

2. Read a compelling section from the book.

    ". . . while the car started to sway, but I wasn't sure if it was me gettin' dizzy or if the car was weaving across the expressway. At the time it seemed really funny. We was laughin' so hard—especially when people started honkin' at us. The more they tried to signal us, and I guess, warn us, the more we was crackin' up and laughin'. Rob had his feet up on the dashboard, partly actin' silly, and partly 'cause his legs was so long that they got cramped in that little car of Andy's. Me and B. J. was in the back-seat. I was sittin' right behind Andy, and B. J. was sittin' next to me, behind Rob, 'cause he had the shortest legs, and Rob could push the seat all the way back.

Then, all of a sudden, like outta nowhere, this wall was in front of us, like it just jumped out in front of the car, and Andy was trying to find the brakes with his foot, and then there was glass everywhere and this crunchin', grindin' sound. My door flew open, and I rolled out. I remember I was cryin' and crawlin' around on my hands and knees." (Draper 1996, 12–13)

3. Tell a little about the book to tease kids' interest.

> "*Tears of a Tiger*, told from several points of view, begins with the accident and proceeds to describe the guilt of the driver, Andy Jackson, who survived. This is his story from the accident until . . . well, find out by reading the book."

4. Finally, give some questions to help scaffold the reading (Foster 2002).

   - Is Andy's story believable?
   - What should the parents have done differently?
   - Do you agree with the way school officials reacted? Explain.
   - Did Andy's girlfriend give him support and comfort? Explain.
   - How have people you have known reacted to similar situations?

During our book talks, kids had whispered exchanges. "Oh, that one sounds good. I want to read that one." "My friend also said that book was cool. I think I'll read that book." Tutors were enthusiastic and knowledgeable about the books, giving only enough information to make the kids want to read. It was entertaining to watch the tutors try to win over the kids. We could feel the competitive vibes in the air.

After the presentations, the tutors gave kids a chance to look through books, which were displayed on five separate tables. Kids read back covers, flipped through and read passages, and discussed books with their friends and tutors. It was refreshing to see high school kids get excited about books, and we knew it was because we had chosen appealing books that related to them. Yet we knew it wouldn't be easy; these kids didn't have a strong desire to read. Many students read at below-grade levels, and even if we gave them books that intrigued them, there was no guarantee they would sit down and read them or be able to read them with understanding.

Literature Circles

On reading workshop days, students work in groups of about six each based on the books they are reading. The workshop includes a prereading minilesson followed by twenty minutes of reading. The postreading discussions, sharing, journal writing, or help with comprehension closely follow the schedule suggested by Harvey Daniels (2002), an expert in literature circles.

The time spent reading is amazing. Everyone reads: high school students, tutors, the teacher. The first time we experienced the electric silence, we were very happily surprised. We had heard so many horror stories about sustained silent reading, so many nightmares. We were able to feel the kids reading because we were reading too. There was nothing else to do. However, it was very hard for the high school students to finish the book during class time, and very few of them read at home.

One of the tutors who studied Daniels' book very carefully made the following recommendations for future reading workshops.

> I recommend you use sticky notes to mark ideas in your books, ideas that connect to you or puzzle you or bother you [Daniels 2002, 67–68]. When all students in the group are responsible for responding to the text (even if they only have four or five sticky notes full of information per meeting) the discussion can last for at least twenty minutes. In twenty minutes, a teacher can check in with each group of students at least twice. In order to have a discussion, the students have to have the time to read in class; there is simply no other way to be sure that a student is reading. It is not a bad idea to get discussions started with one of your own personal connections. Read the passage out loud to the students, share your connection, and model a way to ask other group members if they agree or have similar points to mention. The key to keeping literature circle/reading workshops under control is meticulous organization that includes checkpoint accountability for every part of the group meeting. Each meeting should follow a similar schedule created by the teacher. For example, each student must share all of his or her connections at the beginning of a meeting, and the students must include all of the sticky notes in a group folder or their work portfolio. (Sharon Greenblatt, interview, July 13, 2007)

Minilessons in the Reading Workshop

Usually, tutors teach for the first ten or fifteen minutes of the workshop. They are free to develop their own lessons as long as they work on a reading strategy to help students with comprehension; many of them base their lessons on the strategies developed by

Kylene Beers (2003). These minilessons deal with prereading, reading, and postreading activities, many of them involving graphic organizers. Figure 3.1 is an example of a Venn diagram we used to help students connect with (by visually seeing) the differences and similarities between one of their favorite characters in *The Pact* and themselves.

Most minilessons involve tutors modeling the strategy with their own book, showing kids how they can adapt the technique to fit the book they're reading, and then giving students a handout that provides an example, tips, and questions. Beers (2003) recommends using poetry to teach comprehension strategies (114) and using bookmarks as a scaffolding strategy (130–32). The bookmark shown in Figure 3.2 is a homework assignment that didn't pertain just to kids who were reading *The Pact*. We used some lyrics written by a rapper whom the kids loved, Tupac, to inspire them to listen to music like they would read a poem and write their own interpretations of a song of their choice.

Beers (2003) writes, "There are multiple ways to help students improve their comprehending abilities. Some of these ways are less explicit; others are more explicit" (36). We used the explicit scaffolding aid in Figure 3.3, another bookmark idea, to help students comprehend the themes of *I Know Why the Caged Bird Sings*. The strategy in Figure 3.4 helps students make personal and literary connections to the book.

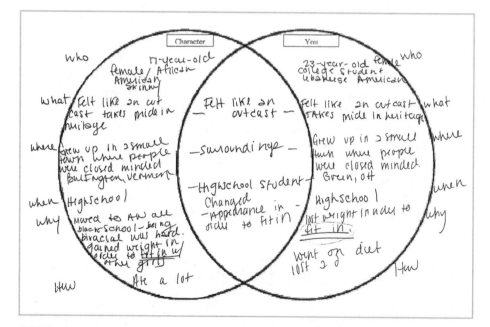

FIGURE 3.1 *Venn Diagram to Help Students Connect with the Text*

"Even if you weren't from the inner-city, if you listened to Tupac, you got the feeling that the thugs have more heart than you thought. He reached into himself and tried to interpret where a lot of the negative behavior came from, and he crafted his lyrics in a way that you could really understand" (*The Pact*, p. 159).

Tupac's songs give listeners insight into his troubled life: the violence, racism, and poverty he experienced and saw. Words are powerful. Examine the lyrics of a song that has impacted you.

For homework:

1. Write the title of the song and the lyrics on a sheet of paper.
2. The song cannot contain profane language but can discuss controversial issues such as racism, discrimination, war, abortion, poverty.
3. Write an essay about your interpretation of the song. Explain why it is powerful to you, what makes the lyrics meaningful, and discuss the singer's message.
4. Find a picture that expresses the message of the song and attach it to your essay and lyric sheet.
5. Your essay must be at least one page, double-spaced, 12 pt. font.

FIGURE 3.2 *Bookmark About* The Pact

Strategies like these give the tutors real insights into how the students see the books they are reading and what connections they make. As Beers (2003) writes, "We must teach [students] strategies that will help them understand texts" (41). For example, Artis wrote about *I Know Why the Caged Bird Sings*:

> Ways that I am caged are poverty. The way I sing is by being an individual and doing my best to work out of it by saving 10% of every dollar that I make so that someday I can buy my own restaurant and build my own empire.

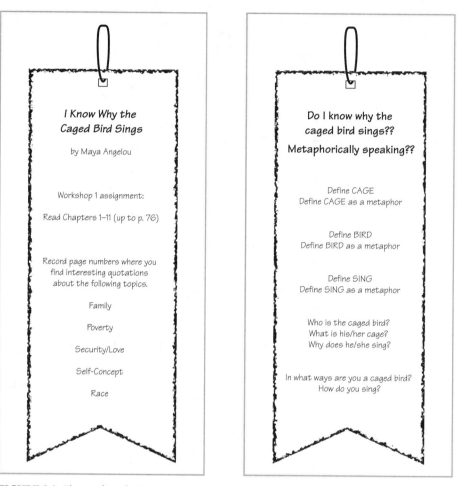

FIGURE 3.3 *First Bookmark About*
I Know Why the Caged Bird Sings

FIGURE 3.4 *Second Bookmark About*
I Know Why the Caged Bird Sings

Another Galway student saw herself as a caged bird because of the strictness of her guardian, her aunt. This student claimed she wanted to sing by getting her mom back. Another student wrote: "I am caged because of being in school."

Figure 3.5 lists potential topics for reading workshop minilessons.

▪ Reflecting on Our First Reading Workshop: Don't Give Up

Before we knew it that first year of our reading workshop, Thanksgiving had arrived. Classes were canceled because of holiday assemblies and Thanksgiving vacation.

Other Topics for Reading Workshop Minilessons

- Finding a book that fits you

- Figuring out themes

- Keeping characters straight (characterization)

- Keeping book journals

- Dialogue journaling with classmates

- Getting into a book club

- Finding good books—fiction, nonfiction, biographies, etc.

- Reviewing bestseller lists

- Understanding a difficult book

- Coping with beginnings, middles, and ends

- Helping with reading comprehension strategies

- Providing metacognition strategies

- Working with story pyramids

- Understanding foreshadowing

- Understanding point of view

- Understanding symbolism

- Understanding plot

- Understanding climax and conclusion

- Understanding character conflicts

- Writing a book review

- Writing book notes

- Participating in literature discussion circles

- Learning literature discussion rules

- Creating character baseball cards

- Experiencing poetry that connects to a character, conflict, or book

- Experiencing author biographies

FIGURE 3.5 *Other Topics for Reading Workshop Minilessons*

© 2008 by Harold M. Foster and Megan C. Nosol. From *America's Unseen Kids: Teaching English/Language Arts in Today's Forgotten High Schools*. Portsmouth, NH: Heinemann.

Reading workshop was being pushed aside. As Fridays came and went, tutors noticed a decrease in student reading, motivation, and attention. With four weeks until Christmas break, reading workshop slowly dwindled away. More and more students began to "forget" their books and leave their work in their cars and lockers. By the end of the semester, nearly half the class was reading articles. The first time we do a unit, it doesn't take long for us to see problems. But no one had any ideas about how to turn things around. There had been some successes, but we had failed to bring reading workshop to a satisfying conclusion.

On reflection, we realized that devoting one day per week for reading comprehension and silent reading is not enough to build student enthusiasm, vocabulary, and comprehension. (This is why we later instituted a two-week reading workshop unit.) But we weren't going to give up on improving attitudes about reading and reading comprehension scores. We focused on the next semester and what we thought needed changing.

- Closure, closure, closure! With students choosing one book from a list of five, we could easily create a closure assignment that requires students to finish the book, analyze what they read, and synthesize their knowledge into a presentation in which they sell the book to the class or show why they don't recommend it.
- What do we do if kids don't bring in their books? We thought about bringing in copies of short reading selections to give to students who forget their books. But what does this accomplish in the end? Students know that what they are reading is temporary and has no connection to the book they are reading; thus, they won't put much effort into reading that day. Well, what about keeping extra copies of books in class? No, what we really need to do is hold kids accountable for bringing in the books they are reading. We decided to give points to the kids who do.
- When is the best time to have silent reading, and how much of it is enough to improve comprehension? Most of our kids refuse to read outside the classroom, so asking them to read their books at home is futile. Yet is giving kids ten minutes a day, at the beginning or end of class time, really enough? Maybe devoting a block of two or three weeks to reading books in the classroom might do the trick.

Based on our start-up problems, we created the checklist shown in Figure 3.6 to help us organize and prepare for a reading workshop. We use it to remind us of the essential elements we need to think about and prepare for.

Our reading workshop still isn't perfect. Then again, what unit is? Lessons always need to change, adapt, and evolve. Change is inevitable and a good thing in teaching. It is valuable to rethink units. We need the courage to reflect on mistakes, to be hon-

Reading Workshop Plan and Checklist

1. Get to know the students' reading habits and reading interests. (Perhaps develop a reading inventory questionnaire.)

2. Find five books that match the students' reading interests. Here are a few things to think about to make sure a book will work.
   a. Can enough copies of the book be gathered?
   b. Consider the average reading level of the class. Is the book below, at, or above the class reading level?
   c. Will the book be challenging enough to students to push them to improve their reading skills?
   d. Will the characters, plot, and themes of the books interest the students?
   e. Will the students be able to relate to the characters and their problems?

3. Read the books again, becoming very familiar with each one. Design the reading workshop ahead of time to be sure there is enough time. If you have tutors to help you, divide the books among them, and have them read the books and try to sell them to the students. "Making the match between book and reader relies on knowledge in three areas: knowing the reader, knowing the book, and knowing the techniques for bringing book and reader together" (Lesesne 2003, 1).

4. Design minilessons. Be flexible; adjust the lessons to fit students' needs. Have extra minilessons prepared just in case. It doesn't hurt to be overprepared.
   a. Decide what kinds of minilessons will help students connect to their books (characterization, themes, foreshadowing, symbolism, etc.).
   b. Also decide what kinds of reading strategies to teach (e.g., KWL charts).

5. Create a final project that will get students to analyze and write about their books. It should be a general topic that any student with any book can do. This should be given to students either at the beginning of the unit or shortly thereafter so that students know what is expected of them.

6. Don't forget about assessment. Attach percentages or weights to each homework assignment, quiz, minilesson, and final project. Give students a copy of the assessment plan within the first week so they know what to expect. For example:

   Bringing books to class: 1 point
   Reading when directed: 1 point
   Group discussion: 2 points
   Journaling: 2 points
   Total of 6 points each workshop

7. Make sure each student has the book he or she wants to read. Devote a class period to giving book presentations to the kids and then allow them time to discuss their choices and select their books.

8. After recording student book choices, assign literature circles for the unit. Ideally, students should be in groups of four, five, or six (Daniels 2002).

9. Have a plan for when things go wrong. Think about what to do when a student forgets his or her book, what to do when a student isn't reading or dislikes a book, and how to handle discipline issues that arise during reading sessions.

FIGURE 3.6 *Reading Workshop Plan and Checklist*

est about the problems in the unit, and to not give up on good ideas that could use a little tweaking.

■ Megan and the Girl Who Fell Through the Cracks

Some students begged to take their books home. Others finished one book and went immediately on to the next.

Emily read five books that semester.

Jake and Drew recommended their books to classmates.

Of course, we also had students like Jeremy and Leslie, who sent text messages to each other on their cell phones when they were supposed to be reading, but we redirected them.

Then there was Alisha, three or four reading levels below her grade.

When the students selected books as a class, Alisha was absent and consequently missed out on listening to the book talks. Since I worked with Alisha regularly, Hal asked me to introduce Alisha to the books when she returned to class the following Monday. Having read only the Angelou book myself, I collected book summaries from other tutors so I could give Alisha a fair description of all of them. Slouched in her desk, with her left arm bent to support her head, she looked completely detached from my shtick. *Remember how uninterested you were in high school, Megan,* I kept reminding myself. I decided to try a different approach.

"Okay, Alisha, what kinds of books do you like to read? Fiction, biography, nonfiction?" I asked, trying to be patient and sympathetic.

"I don't like to read. Can't I just sit in silence and do homework during reading time?" she said in an apathetic tone.

"No, everyone has a book to read, including me, so let's go to the library and select a book together," I said, gently pulling her out of her seat and leading her to the library.

I had the same ambivalence about reading in high school. I don't think one day of walking through a maze of books with a college girl would have modified my state of mind. Nearly half the class period was wasted as Alisha wondered aimlessly around the library, distracted by friends she ran into.

"Pick out a book that appeals to you, Alisha. Anything you want," I said.

I figured that reading was reading, so the only imperative was that Alisha read. In the end, she chose a book about a group of middle school girls dealing with crushes, gossip, and parents. I wasn't thrilled—it was at the seventh-grade level—but I allowed it as long as she promised to read during class periods. I was happy that we at least left the library that day with a book.

I started thinking about the other kids in class and whether I had helped Alisha at all that day. *Am I being fair to the other students by allowing Alisha to stray from the reading selection? Did I make the right decision about giving Alisha a lower-level, simplistic book to read? Did I avoid confronting Alisha's reading problems altogether?*

But Alisha would have gotten lost trying to decipher meaning and vocabulary during the small amount of time allotted to reading each week. Although Alisha's book problem wasn't a life-or-death situation, improving Alisha's reading skills was vital to her education and future. Everything a teacher does in the classroom has an effect on students, and I worried that I was too easy on her.

Ah, yes, the "butterfly effect." The theory that every person in this world has the power to impact another person, and that person has the ability to continue the cycle by touching another life, and so on.

With twenty tutors working in our classroom, Alisha should have been given extra attention so that she could read a book from the reading selection, but at her own pace. A tutor could have worked with Alisha during reading periods. But we just didn't have enough time. A semester wasn't enough time in which to transform Alisha into a strategic reader. A long time ago, Alisha should have been sent to special education teachers to address her reading problems. *But where were these special education teachers? Why was Alisha reading books four levels below her level? Alisha fell through the cracks a long time ago*, I kept thinking.

I could have fallen through the cracks too when I was in high school, but I had parents who helped me develop reading habits and some teachers who "sold" me books through their exciting and thought-provoking class discussions. I have a feeling that teachers gave up on Alisha, who was passed from grade to grade.

Alisha's situation made me sad and mad.

What was I supposed to do with a student who was expected to pass eleventh-grade reading tests, college entrance exams, and college courses but couldn't comprehend texts past the eighth-grade reading level? I wasn't a reading specialist, but I knew I could read with her and help her with words and comprehension.

I sat with Alisha on Fridays, reading my book next to hers. Most days, I took her out in the hallway and asked her to read passages from her book. I asked her questions, and we discussed the plot. But I could tell that Alisha wasn't being challenged. She needed a book that was a little above her reading level but that dealt with more complex issues.

One day after class, I talked to Hal about my dilemma. It was the third week of our reading workshop; Alisha was reading but not being pushed beyond her limits. Hal mentioned *Speak*, by Laurie Halse Anderson, and *The Outsiders*, by S. E. Hinton. I had heard rave reviews about *Speak*, so I grabbed a copy from his shelf and began reading some excerpts. By the end of the night, after reading a few passages in the book, I decided to persuade Alisha to change books the next day. It seemed to be slightly above her reading level, but the vocabulary is simple, and I thought Alisha could relate to the main character, Melinda.

Speak was a hard sell. Alisha looked at the book's cover as if she were reviewing a dented car on clearance. "No thanks."

"Give it a chance. I know once you start reading it, you won't be able to put the book down," I pleaded.

This is where having a good relationship with a student comes in handy.

I think Alisha took the book only to appease me, but we began reading it together that day. She read a page or two and I read a paragraph or two until we stopped at an interesting section of the chapter to chat.

But *Speak* came to Alisha too late in the semester.

Alisha was a puzzle I had a hard time piecing together. I felt she needed more help than I, or even Sally, could ever give her. After working with Alisha a few times, I noticed she had difficulty reading, comprehending what she was reading, and writing a proper sentence. Often, she wrote some of her letters backward. I knew she wore glasses because of vision problems, but I was beginning to think it was much more than just vision problems. Sure, it's not uncommon for kids to struggle with reading comprehension, but when a student is reading a piece of literature a few grades below her and still having problems pronouncing words and writing a whole sentence, there's a problem. Two more years of high school wasn't enough to prepare her for college. She needed outside help.

But Sally saw Alisha's situation differently. She said that involving special education teachers would worsen Alisha's problems at home and that it wasn't something she wanted to do.

I didn't understand. (It seemed so simple to me at the time, but looking back, I see that students like Alisha are a major dilemma for any teacher.)

I respected Sally as a teacher and knew she was good to these kids, but I thought Alisha's problems in school far outweighed the reasons not to involve her parents. However, Sally didn't want to accuse Alisha of having learning problems for fear she was wrong. She knew Alisha had low confidence in herself already, and she thought that getting her tested for learning disabilities would shatter her completely. Plus, a teacher must get the parent's permission to request a learning evaluation of a student, and Sally wasn't comfortable doing that. Alisha's parents had had many battles with the school, and from talking with Alisha I knew she was afraid of her stepdad's temper.

One day, I decided to talk to Hal about Alisha's academic problems. I was angry that Sally wasn't doing anything about them, and I begged him to join me in talking to Sally about getting Alisha outside help.

The next afternoon, Hal and I asked Sally if we could talk to her after class. I told her about Alisha's reading and writing problems. Sally walked calmly into the hallway and asked Alisha to step back inside the classroom for a moment.

"Alisha, can you read this?" Sally pointed to a paragraph in an English literature anthology she pulled from her classroom shelf.

"Sure," Alisha replied, proceeding to read silently and slowly.

"Can you tell me what you just read about, please?" asked Sally.

Alisha answered briefly, providing very little information.

"Thank you. You can leave now." Sally closed the book and returned it to the shelf.

"I think that answers your questions about Alisha, right?" she said after Alisha had gone.

I was speechless. *What kind of evaluation was that?* I looked at Hal, a baffled look on my face. A seventh grader could have given the same elusive answer. Yet, somehow, that was good enough for Sally.

That was it. Case closed. I left Sally's classroom that day filled with questions that I have never been able to answer. I remember wondering how many kids in my future classrooms will be allowed for some reason to fall through the cracks of our educational system. The big question is, what is a teacher to do? With only two more years left of high school, and one more semester to spend with Alisha, what should Sally have done? What will I do when I encounter an Alisha in my classroom?

Hal's Response: Too Little, Too Late

Sally felt that Alisha's central problems were not skills but psychological issues. On the other hand, Megan, who worked closely with Alisha, felt she was so far behind because of years of neglect, her low self-esteem, and her lack of motivation. The help we offered, as far as we could tell, did not work for Alisha. As Megan states, it was too little, too late. As far as we know, we did not improve her skills, give her more confidence, or help her in any way we could discern. Megan may have been right to wonder why Alisha was not given special help by trained professionals who truly understood the issues. Are there problems that are beyond the knowledge of most English teachers, and did Alisha have those kinds of problems? Or, as Sally thought, would we have just made it worse by convincing Alisha that her learning problems were so severe she needed special attention? A tough call that teachers must make all the time.

Figure 3.7 shows a list of books that could be useful for reading workshops.

Recommended Multicultural Literature for Adolescents

Books About African Americans

A Lesson Before Dying, by Ernest J. Gaines

And Still We Rise: The Trials and Triumphs of Twelve Gifted Inner-City Students, by Miles Corwin

And This Too Shall Pass, by E. Lynn Harris

Beating the Odds, by Freeman A. Hrabowski, Kenneth I. Maton, and Geoffrey L. Greif

Beloved, by Toni Morrison

Disappearing Acts, by Terry McMillan

Go Tell It on the Mountain, by James Baldwin

Hope in the Unseen: An American Odyssey from the Inner City to the Ivy League, by Ron Suskind

Invisible Man, by Ralph Ellison

Native Son, by Richard Wright

Our America: Life and Death on the South Side of Chicago, by LeAlan Jones and Lloyd Newman, with David Isay

Some Love, Some Pain, Some Time: Stories, by J. California Cooper

Song of Solomon, by Toni Morrison

Stories of Scottsboro, by James Goodman

The Autobiography of Malcolm X, by Alex Haley and Malcolm X

The Beast, by Walter Dean Meyers

The Big Picture, by Ben Carson, with Gregg Lewis

The Bluest Eye, by Toni Morrison

The Cay, by Theodore Taylor

The Color Purple, by Alice Walker

The First Part Last, by Angela Johnson

The Watsons Go to Birmingham—1963, by Christopher Paul Curtis

Their Eyes Were Watching God, by Zora Neale Hurston

There Are No Children Here, by Alex Kotlowitz

Popular Authors of African American Literature

Connie Briscoe

Octavia Butler

Popular Authors of African American Literature, *continued*

Bebe Moore Campbell

Eric Jerome Dickey

Albert French

Ernest Gaines

Nikki Giovanni

Alex Haley

Chester Himes

Langston Hughes

Sheneska Jackson

Angela Johnson

Walter Mosley

Gloria Naylor

Omar Tyree

Asian and Pacific Islander Literature

American Eyes: New Asian American Short Stories for Young Adults, by Lori Carlson

Believers in America: Poems About Americans of Asian and Pacific Islander Descent, by Steven Izuki and illustrated by Bill Fukuda McCoy

Donald Duk, by Frank Chin

Mona in the Promised Land, by Gish Jen

Necessary Roughness, by Marie G. Lee

Shadow of the Dragon, by Sherry Garland

Snow Falling on Cedars, by David Guterson

The Clay Marble, by Minfong Ho

The Joy Luck Club, by Amy Tan

Hispanic Literature

Bless Me, Ultima, by Rudolfo A. Anaya

Taking Sides, by Gary Soto

The Alchemist, by Paul Coelho

The House on Mango Street, by Sandra Cisneros

Native American Literature

Spirit Walker, by Nancy Wood

The Grass Dancer, by Susan Power

The Shadow Brothers, by A. E. Cannon

Tracks, by Louise Erdrich

FIGURE 3.7 *Recommended Multicultural Literature for Adolescents*

Teaching Shakespeare in the Urban Classroom | 4

▪ Why Shakespeare?

Shakespeare may be perceived as just one more white, establishment author far removed from the experiences of our African American kids at Galway. However, that's like saying that Hal, a white male, has no business reading the plays of August Wilson, a black playwright, whose plays Hal dearly loves. In the suburbs, kids read Lorraine Hansberry, author of *A Raisin in the Sun*, and Shakespeare. To deny Galway students the curriculum we give our suburban students is a form of discrimination. Let the Galway students rail against the place of Shakespeare in our culture, but let them fight from an intelligent position after having read and understood him.

During the first year of the project, when Hal told his student-teacher tutors they would be teaching *A Midsummer Night's Dream* to the Galway students, they rebelled.

"These kids can't read well enough."

"Shakespeare has no relevance for these kids."

"They won't want to read the work of a dead white man."

"What's the point of teaching them something they don't want to read or won't understand?"

Two months later, after the tutors had formed relationships with Galway students and all the stereotypes had been shattered, Hal asked them if they were ready to teach Shakespeare to Sally's class. They enthusiastically replied, "Let's go for it!" They had realized Galway students had the capability of understanding and appreciating

Shakespeare, and they also felt confident enough to challenge the high schoolers. After weeks of working with Galway students, they recognized the kids' potential.

One of the African American tutors had in fact noted firsthand the difference in the quality of the literature she read when she went to a city high school and the books her friends in a suburban high school read. She was convinced that her teachers felt she and her classmates weren't bright enough for certain literary works, that only suburban kids had the ability to read difficult literature. She was determined this stereotype not be perpetuated with Galway's urban students.

Thus was born the teaching unit that ended each semester during the nine years of our collaboration with Galway. The play was always *A Midsummer Night's Dream*, except for one amazing and successful unit on *King Lear*. But that's another story. *A Midsummer Night's Dream* works well in the classroom because it is an ensemble play; no Hamlet or Macbeth takes over. It's also a comedy that lets us laugh *with* the characters instead of *at* them when they make mistakes.

The Shakespeare unit is a performance-based project Hal includes in his Teaching Adolescent Literature course. The goal of the unit is to produce a readers theater production of the play. His student teachers are equipped with a full set of lessons, scaffolds, and approaches (which apply to any complex, dramatic work, whether it's by Shakespeare, Lorraine Hansberry, or August Wilson).

Shakespeare is culturally relevant to anyone who experiences the difficulties of establishing and maintaining loving relationships. Our project is about transforming the curriculum for nontracked urban students by providing an enriched, engaging, holistic, and intelligent curriculum. It is entirely possible to make Shakespeare meaningful and motivational, and that is exactly what we do with our performance-based approach.

By the end of our Shakespeare unit, our at-risk students are able to:

- connect with a major work of literature
- comprehend a complex and classic literary work
- experience the gratification of reading a difficult text successfully
- feel the satisfaction of completing an advanced curriculum unit

Planning This Complex Project

Shakespeare can be an overwhelming unit to teach.

- Students are afraid of Shakespeare.
- Students lack motivation.
- Students have trouble understanding Shakespearean language.
- The plot, themes, and characters are complex.
- Coordinating a meaningful performance is hard, exhausting work.

In our project's unit, the tutors responsible for teaching it have two and a half weeks to teach *A Midsummer Night's Dream* and put on a readers theater production of the play in the school's auditorium. The relatively brief time line is challenging. To give themselves a fighting chance, the tutors put together a planning calendar, divide the lessons among themselves, and use a preparation checklist (see Figure 4.1).

Because we wanted each student to have a copy of the edited version of the play that could be marked up as necessary, tutors downloaded a complete copy of the play from the Internet (legally, since Shakespeare is in the public domain), created an edited version, and had copies duplicated. We cut most of the mystical sections with their complex illusions and imagery that don't connect to the lives of the students. We also eliminated Act IV, which lacks the broad humor and deep melodrama found in the rest of the play. (Unfortunately, this meant sacrificing the wonderful speech Bottom makes about his "dream.")

Since Shakespeare is the last unit of the semester, there's no way to "borrow" more time at the end. Tutors need to get down to business and create a snappy unit that moves quickly and includes:

- fun, interactive lessons that help familiarize students with the language and the play's plot
- ways for students to connect to the play authentically and meaningfully
- scaffolding to help students comprehend the play

Megan and Shakespeare

Romeo and Juliet, Julius Caesar, Antony and Cleopatra, and *King Lear* all bored me and my classmates to death when I was in high school. My English teachers tried to make Shakespeare "enjoyable" by assigning parts and having us read aloud, but we refused to participate, pretended to listen, fell asleep, and daydreamed big time. Our faces mainly conveyed confusion. How could anyone find Shakespeare's plays fun while sitting at a desk and listening to other people casually read the lines? Year after year, Shakespeare became more and more mind-numbing as I sat waiting for my turn to read a few lines.

Looking back, I understand why I didn't participate during the Shakespeare units and why I had no desire to read the plays in high school. The way my English teachers approached Shakespeare was so teacher-centered that the students felt alienated, left out. It was these botched experiences with Shakespeare in high school and my lack of motivation to read anything, let alone Shakespeare, that made me determined to stay as far away as I could from any Shakespeare class in college.

But there was no escaping the Bard.

Preparation Checklist	Yes
1. Select a high-quality play around which to anchor the unit (the original words, no editing).	
2. Decide on student learning goals for the unit (lesson objectives).	
3. Develop a unit calendar based on unit objectives and lessons.	
4. Schedule in-class and out-of-class assignments (minilessons, group work, homework, rehearsals, etc.).	
5. Create a planning matrix.	
6. Develop an assessment plan to measure student performance (quizzes, papers, exams, performance, etc., a percentage of the final grade assigned to each).	
7. Edit the script for classroom performance and make copies for students. Pick the scenes that . . . • have a strong connection to your students • involve action • a modern audience will find funny, dramatic, and exciting • have accessible language (easy to mildly difficult lines) Omit scenes that . . . • lack direction • do not add to the overall message or theme of the play Omit characters who . . . • show up for less than a page • have no connection to the central conflict • are used as technical devices and are never seen or heard of again (e.g., a waiter who takes an order)	
8. Assign roles based on students' personalities.	
9. Gather appropriate props.	
10. Choose a location for performance (classroom, auditorium, etc.).	
11. Group students according to the act(s) in which they appear.	
12. Designate a group leader for each act.	
13. Create a printed program if outsiders (other classes, parents, etc.) will attend.	

FIGURE 4.1 *Preparation Checklist*

As an English major, I was required to take Shakespeare classes. Worse, he consistently popped up in many of my non-Shakespeare English classes. But even my most enthusiastic professors couldn't change my attitude toward our world's most renowned playwright.

When I got involved with the Galway High School collaboration, I knew I was going to have to teach one unit to the eleventh graders. On the sign-up sheet, I avoided the Shakespeare unit like the plague. Instead, assuming it was a better fit, I signed up to teach persuasive writing. After Hal reviewed the sign-up sheet, he said he needed someone to join the two brave souls in the Shakespeare group. "Megan? How about you?" My memories of high school Shakespeare racing through my mind, I cringed. *Hal,* I thought to myself, *you really don't want me on the Shakespeare unit. I'm terrible at Shakespeare!*

But I was Hal's graduate assistant. I agreed.

As a teacher-in-training, I knew how to prepare a lesson, but I didn't have much experience building an entire unit. I had devised units in my education classes, sure, but I was never able to test them on real students. The summer before I had taken Hal's Teaching Adolescent Literature class, so I had a structure from which to work. Nevertheless, I was nervous; I wasn't sure I could make Shakespeare interesting and enjoyable for Galway students who, like me, were turned off by Shakespeare and rarely if ever had a positive experience with his plays.

I tried to think of all the things my high school English teachers should have done to make Shakespeare more successful for me—thought-provoking, interactive lessons that could help me make sense of Shakespeare and his plays. Where my high school teachers had failed most was in helping me and my classmates connect the universal themes of Shakespeare's plays—the characters and their conflicts—with our own relationships and problems. Teachers make *A Midsummer Night's Dream* meaningful to students when they tap into the students' real-life experiences with love triangles and unyielding parents.

As I helped the Galway students make sense of the language and the story, I learned that one of the best ways to make Shakespeare's plays fun and accessible is through readers theater. Plays aren't novels; they are written as dialogue and become much more comprehensible to readers when they speak and act out the lines.

■ Dealing with Language Issues: Megan's Swearing Game

The year Megan participated in the project, she taught the first lesson in the Shakespeare unit. She needed to introduce *A Midsummer Night's Dream* captivatingly enough for the kids to want to learn more. These eleventh graders had already been exposed to Shakespeare and his plays. Chances were they loathed reading them, just as Megan

had in high school. So she wanted to give them a light-hearted, comical introduction that dealt with the language and humor of the play and instantly sparked interest, enthusiasm, and motivation.

Taking ideas from Peggy O'Brien, author of *Shakespeare Set Free* (1993), and adapting O'Brien's lessons to her own teaching style, Megan turned her first lesson into an Insult Improv game (see Figures 4.2 and 4.3) as a way to familiarize kids with the language and ease their fears about standing up in front of an audience and reading difficult lines.

After a weekend of development and practice, Megan felt prepared. She had looked at the game from all angles. She had brainstormed all the problems that could come up and planned ahead. She had recruited her sister, a high school student, as a guinea pig for the teenager point of view. (She also began to realize how overwhelming teaching could easily become. She couldn't imagine doing this for every lesson.)

Megan set up the classroom before the students rolled in. Her coteachers, Alex and Erin, greeted students at the door, and Erin divided the class into two equal teams. When everyone was seated, Megan read the class the directions of the game and then modeled it for them.

Once Sally, the tutors, and the most outgoing students participated, the quiet kids began to get involved. Mike, a student who had recently arrived from Liberia, surprised us all when he was persuaded to give it a shot. He showed his classmates another side of himself, saying his line with a dramatic sense of humor in his British accent. Portia, the most outspoken girl in our class, energetically insulted him right back. Shakespeare was being spewed, yelled, screamed, and cried, with attitude and comprehension. The class spilled over into the next period. Megan taught a better Shakespeare lesson than she had ever experienced as a student.

Shakespeare Unit
Insult Improv Game

A. Overall Statement

This is a fun game designed to introduce students to Shakespeare's language.

B. Goals

- to familiarize students with Shakespeare and his language
- to practice fluency in reading Shakespeare out loud
- to get students to apply reading comprehension strategies through translating Shakespearean language into modern language
- to help students become more comfortable with speaking in front of an audience

C. Objectives

1. acquisition of vocabulary
2. reading process: concepts of print, comprehension strategies, and self-monitoring strategies
3. communication: oral and visual

D. Materials Needed

- insults (on pieces of paper)
- a box to hold the insults
- candy (one general bag of candy and three special pieces of candy)
- scorecards
- "awards" paper

E. Procedure Steps

Give directions to the class:

1. Introduce the game to the class:

   "Shakespeare is known for some very impressive, funny insults. Today, we're going to play a game that will help you get comfortable with reading and speaking Shakespeare in front of an audience. Don't worry, you will not be graded on your acting ability! Judges will base their opinions on enthusiasm, effort, and entertainment value. Here's how Insult Improv is played. . . ."

2. Divide the class into two teams, The Fools and The Dumb Show (mix college tutors and Galway students), and put them on opposite sides of the room.

3. Explain to the class who the fools are in Shakespeare and the concept of a dumb show.

continues

FIGURE 4.2 *Directions for the Shakespeare Insult Improv Game*

E. Procedure Steps, *continued*

4. Tell the class, "One person from each side will come up to the front of the room and blindly take a piece of paper from the box. This paper will have a Shakespearean insult written on it. Once the student sees the paper, she cannot show it to or speak to anyone else but the teacher in charge."

5. Tell the students that they will have a few seconds to quietly read the insult and figure out how they're going to say it in front of the class. If students have any questions about the words, remind them to privately ask the teacher in charge.

6. The object of the game is to see which side can insult best.

7. Students can insult the other person in many ways—they can read the insult in another voice, scream it, cry it, act it out with props, or make it funny.

8. The three judges selected from the college tutors and high school students will vote on which person expressed the insult best.

   - Anyone who volunteers to come up in front of the class and insult will get a piece of candy and participation points.
   - The student who wins an insult round gets a point for his or her team.
   - The winner will have an opportunity to get another piece of candy for translating the insult into modern English—no cusswords, please.
   - The team with the most points at the end of twenty minutes will get bonus points.
   - If there is a tie at the end of twenty minutes, each team will pick one person to represent the team and do one more insult match for the judges.

9. If time permits, the class can vote on the most creative, the funniest, and the meanest insulters. Winners will get a special prize.

10. Pass out pieces of paper and ask students to vote.

Summary/Conclusion

This activity will, we hope, accomplish our three objectives by getting students (either volunteers or chosen students) to go in front of the class, read their Shakespeare insults, and translate the meanings of the insults. This activity is fun and educational because students will become more comfortable with reading difficult text aloud and in front of an audience as they watch other students, including the college students, read Shakespeare.

FIGURE 4.2 *Continued*

© 2008 by Harold M. Foster and Megan C. Nosol. From *America's Unseen Kids: Teaching English/Language Arts in Today's Forgotten High Schools*. Portsmouth, NH: Heinemann.

Shakespeare Insults

Tempt not too much the hatred of my spirit, for I am sick when I do look on thee

Hang yourself, you muddy conger, hang yourself

Toads, beetles, bats, light on you

Away, you three-inch fool

What you egg Young fry of treachery

Thou wouldst eat thy dead vomit up

You should be women and yet your beards forbid me to interpret that you are so

Hang, cur! hang, you whoreson, insolent noisemaker

Foot-licker

Breath of garlic-eaters

You vicious mole of nature

Thou art like a toad; ugly and venomous

Thou poisonous bunch-back'd toad

Hang off, thou cat, thou burr! Vile thing, let loose, or I will shake thee from me
    like a serpent

Thine face is not worth sunburning

Go thou and fill another room in hell

Go, prick thy face, and over-red thy fear,
    Thou lily-liver'd boy

Let's meet as little as we can

Go to, you're a dry fool, I'll no more of you

Out, dunghill

Ah, you whoreson loggerhead, you were born to doe me shame

Thou hideous, onion-eyed, rabbit sucker

Hag-seed hence

Dissembling harlot, thou art false in all

Thou art a boil, a plague-sore, an embossed carbuncle in my corrupted blood

I do not like your look, I promise thee

Degenerate and base art thou

Your breath stinks with eating toasted cheese

Die a beggar

More of your conversation would infect my brain

FIGURE 4.3 *Insults for the Shakespeare Insult Improv Game*

© 2008 by Harold M. Foster and Megan C. Nosol. From *America's Unseen Kids: Teaching English/Language Arts in Today's Forgotten High Schools*. Portsmouth, NH: Heinemann.

■ Vygotsky's ZPD: Building a Bridge

Next, the tutors had to provide Galway students with the necessary support to help them work through the play on their own. Part of a teacher's job is to identify students' zone of proximal development (ZPD), a term coined by educational theorist Lev Vygotsky for the state of being in which we are able to understand a concept or perform a task *with help* (Moll 1992). Before determining a student's ZPD, the teacher must first get to know the student—learning style, personality, home life, and academic history. Once this relationship is established, the teacher gets a fuller picture of the student's strengths and weaknesses, the obstacles that hinder the student, and how the student can be helped.

Here's what the tutors discovered.

- The Galway students were capable of reading Shakespeare phonetically without help. This was their zone of actual development (ZAD), or level of independent performance.

- The Galway students were capable of understanding Shakespeare *but needed help to do so*. This put comprehension of the text in the ZPD and became the focus of the lessons.

- The Galway students required *assisted performance*, which the tutors could provide by building a "bridge" connecting the students with the text.

Figure 4.4 lists some common problems that stand in the way of students being able to understand a concept or accomplish a task on their own. For example, if a teacher can eliminate a distraction, connect students to what they are learning, or raise stu-

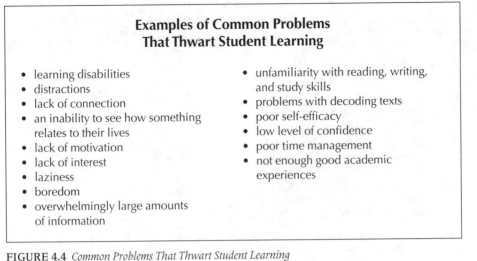

**Examples of Common Problems
That Thwart Student Learning**

- learning disabilities
- distractions
- lack of connection
- an inability to see how something relates to their lives
- lack of motivation
- lack of interest
- laziness
- boredom
- overwhelmingly large amounts of information

- unfamiliarity with reading, writing, and study skills
- problems with decoding texts
- poor self-efficacy
- low level of confidence
- poor time management
- not enough good academic experiences

FIGURE 4.4 *Common Problems That Thwart Student Learning*

dents' confidence, she or he is building a bridge between what the student knows and doesn't know. The Insult Improv is one such motivating and engaging bridge that connects students who enjoy social activities to *A Midsummer Night's Dream*.

▪ Helping Kids Access the Play

After the Insult Improv game, the tutors helped the students tune into the *Midsummer Night's Dream* main characters, many of whom are essentially their age. Becoming familiar with the plot (see the summary handout in Figure 4.5) is necessary at this point, and the tutors did it with these steps.

1. Design bold, colorful nametags for each character, and ask students to wear a character's nametag (character assignments are determined in advance).
2. Divide the class into three groups: the people of the court, the rude mechanicals, and the fairies.
3. Explain how these three groups interact in the play.
4. Tell the story while physically manipulating the characters. For instance, the tutor explaining the opening scene when Hippolyta, the queen of the Amazons, and Theseus discuss their marriage would bring the kids wearing those nametags to the front of the room and move them around in ways appropriate to the action.

The tutors also led class discussions about love triangles, stubborn parents, generation gaps, lack of communication between men and women, unfaithfulness, optimism

A Midsummer Night's Dream
by William Shakespeare

Principal Characters:
    Theseus, Duke of Athens
    Hippolyta, Queen of the Amazons
    Lysander, in love with Hermia
    Demetrius, in love with Hermia
    Hermia, in love with Lysander
    Helena, in love with Demetrius
    Oberon, king of the fairies
    Titania, queen of the fairies
    Puck, fairy page to Oberon
    The rude mechanicals (Bottom, Quince, Flute, etc.)

I. **Act I**
    A. Theseus and Hippolyta plan their wedding.
    B. Hermia and Lysander plan to flee Athens and marry.
    C. Demetrius and Helena plan to follow Lysander and Hermia into the woods.
    D. The rude mechanicals plan their play for the royal wedding.

II. **Act II**
    A. Puck unknowingly anoints the wrong Athenians' eyes: Lysander falls in love with Helena.
    B. Titania's eyes are anointed.

III. **Act III**
    A. The rude mechanicals rehearse their play; Puck changes Bottom's head to an ass' head; Titania falls in love with Bottom.
    B. Demetrius' eyes are anointed, and he falls in love with Helena. Thus, both Lysander and Demetrius love Helena instead of Hermia.

IV. **Act IV**
    A. The love charms are removed (except for Demetrius), and the couples are properly paired.
    B. The lovers think that all that has happened has been but a dream.

V. **Act V**
    A. The three couples are married: Theseus and Hippolyta, Hermia and Lysander, and Helena and Demetrius.
    B. The rude mechanicals perform Pyramus and Thisby.

FIGURE 4.5 *Summary Handout for* A Midsummer Night's Dream

about life, and social status—the fundamental themes of the play. Britney, one of the more reserved Galway girls, spoke about her two friends who were in love with the same guy, and Alisha mentioned her strict parents who never approved of any boyfriend she brought home. Students were exchanging their own life experiences and beginning to connect with the essence of the play in a very personal way.

FIGURE 4.6 A Midsummer Night's Dream *Student Sample*

Before asking students to crack open their scripts, the tutors decided to provide an additional—and unconventional—reference guide: one of them designed a simple ten-page comic book depicting the main scenes of the play (Figure 4.6 shows the first page). These comic books were tedious to put together, but the bridge they provided paid off. Later in the unit, students flipped through them to refresh their memories on a specific scene or act.

▪ Getting Ready to Read

At this point in the unit, Galway students:

- had been dramatically introduced to the language of the play through the Insult Improv activity
- understood the themes of the play by virtue of the open class discussions
- were familiar with the plot of the play from the brief pantomimes of the main scenes, the summary handout, and the comic book

They were well equipped to begin reading the play. Just knowing the plot in advance solves some of the difficulties. Since students know what will happen, they can read the play to appreciate it, feel it, learn it, and own it. Fluency comes that much closer.

Before the tutors started the students on their group work, they led the class in reading selected sections. This can be tedious, but it helps students bridge the gap between the story and the language. It also gives them the big picture. The play comes to life when an enthusiastic teacher asks, "Does Egeus have the right to be so upset when he says, 'Full of vexation come I, with complaint / Against my child, my daughter Hermia'" (1.1.22–23)? This is a teachable moment. A teacher can relate characters' lines to how students feel when battling with their own parents. After Theseus states, "Demetrius is a worthy gentleman" (1.1.52), Hermia gives her mouthy reply, "So is Lysander" (1.1.53). Hermia's modern attitude will connect with every student in the class.

Up to this point, one teacher can present all the activities and lessons. The next step, in which students rehearse scenes in groups, can also be carried out by a single teacher but will be accomplished more effectively with the help of some assistants. All group work involves the same issues:

- students who disagree
- students who rely on others to do the work
- students who readily get off task
- students who misbehave

The built-in advantage of group work in the Shakespeare unit is that each student has a specific job to do—learn about a character, learn how that character contributes to the play, and learn how to read his or her lines with understanding and emotion. The initial scaffolding sets up the rest of the project and makes the difficult job of learning the text doable.

Coaching the Play

After reading selections from the play as a class, the Galway kids rehearsed the following acts and scenes (there were four groups of students, each responsible for one of the acts being performed).

- Act I, Scene 1—Takes place in the court where the conflict starts.
  Scene 2—The rude mechanicals begin to rehearse the play.
- Act II, Scene 1—Demetrius and Helena meet, and their fight is witnessed by the king of the fairies.
  Scene 2—Hermia and Lysander sleep in the woods, and Puck mistakes the sleeping Lysander for Demetrius.
- Act III, Scene 1—Bottom is changed into a donkey, and the bewitched queen of the fairies falls in love with him.
  Scene 2—All of the mistaken identities result in verbal and physical fights among the mortals.
- Act V, Scene 1—All is resolved, and the wedded couples are entertained by the awful play of the rude mechanicals.

The tutors assigned each student a character. Everyone played at least one role, so each act was presented by a different set of students. (Students were assigned more than one part if their role had only a few lines or if they were eager to participate to a greater degree.)

Characters were assigned with the students in mind. Portia was Hermia, since the part required a short girl with an attitude; the reflective Emily played Helena; and Mike was given the part of Egeus because of his height and his willingness to ham it up.

Groups were encouraged to follow the schedule below for the next two weeks.

1. Read through the group scene, just saying the words.
2. Discuss the scene—characterization, motivations, emotions, setting, language, costumes, props.
3. Read the scene with emotion.
4. Block the scene while reading the lines.
5. Review the blocking with some sets and costumes while acting the lines.
6. Rehearse the scene with all sets and costumes.
7. Hold a final dress rehearsal.
8. Perform the scene.

Every day, before teams worked separately, a tutor taught a minilesson summarizing one of the scenes. These minilessons, which were approximately ten minutes long, took many forms: a skit in which the students participated, an unrehearsed reading, a drawing activity, writing prompts. The goal was to connect the students with the scene in question.

■ What Homework? Megan Faces Reality

Homework was something Galway students were not used to: they simply refused to do it. When I told Sally that the other Shakespeare tutors and I had prepared homework assignments, she laughed and said, "My kids will never do that. You're wasting your time."

Another teaching dilemma. What do you do about homework when you have kids who need to work all night or have bad home lives? But I didn't entertain this very valid question until after experiencing Galway.

I couldn't imagine high school without homework. As a high school student, I would have been thrilled and grateful if my teachers had never made me do homework, but that wouldn't have prepared me for the reality of college. I wasn't going to give in so easily. "These kids will have to do things in life that they may not always want to do," I told Hal and my fellow teachers-in-training. Hal looked at me like I was about to climb Mount Everest, but he said, "Give it a try."

He also gave me rules to stick to.

- No selecting quotes from the play and making students translate them into their own words.
- No mindless multiple-choice questions.
- No grammar worksheets that have no connection to the play.
- No character identifications.
- Absolutely no, *no*, **no** crossword puzzles.

- No quizzes on literary terms that students can easily go look up in the dictionary.
- No drills matching characters with speeches.
- No reading and explicating.

I knew better than to use low-level, unfragmented, basic-recall worksheets. From being a student, I was well aware that these activities don't challenge or inspire high schoolers or trigger real learning.

Instead, the group of tutors in charge of the Shakespeare unit wanted to get students to analyze, synthesize, and discuss the play by asking them to write. Our rationale was Benjamin Bloom's *Taxonomy of Educational Objectives* (1956). Bloom and his colleagues recommend that teachers promote higher-order thinking in their classroom lessons so that students think deeply about what they are learning and how they can apply it to their lives. Using questions that encourage this kind of critical thinking, we rightly surmised, would facilitate student comprehension of the play.

Shakespeare wrote about the tragic, comedic, and loving sides of human nature; we hoped students could realize how much they could relate to the themes of *A Midsummer Night's Dream*. Our homework assignments asked students to read each act, analyze it, and write about elements in it that connected to their life experiences. Four simple writing assignments (see Figure 4.7). "Not too much to ask of them, right?" I asked Hal.

But Sally had been right. The moment we uttered the words *homework assignment*, we heard moans and groans emanating from all over the room. Refusing to concede, I handed out the assignment with the directions and an open space that provided students enough room to write their thoughts. Students looked at me blankly, as if they'd never seen a homework assignment before (and they may not have). Some kids stuck the papers randomly in their scripts, others left them untouched on a corner of their desks.

Even though the tutors reminded students that the assignments were an easy five points, a little less than half handed in their homework each day. So maybe Sally wasn't *totally* right. More than one-third of the students did their homework. This could be seen as progress. Perhaps if we continued to maintain high expectations and not give in to the students, more kids would do the assignments and get used to the idea of homework.

Yet what does a teacher do when kids refuse to do their homework? No one can make a student hold the pen and write. Homework gives students an opportunity to apply what they're learning, and we stood by that belief. We gave points to those students who put in effort and thoughtfulness and gave no points to students who didn't do the work. Doing homework needs to be an intrinsic desire for students—they have to *want* to practice. This is why I don't place too much weight on homework anymore, focusing most on having students demonstrate their knowledge through projects and authentic learning applications.

Sample Homework Writing Prompts

1. What did you know about Shakespeare before reading the play? As you continue to read the play, what new things are you learning about Shakespeare? Have your feelings toward Shakespeare and his plays changed at all?

2. Write about your favorite character in *A Midsummer Night's Dream*. What's so interesting about this character? How has he or she changed throughout the course of the play? How have your feelings about this character changed as you read more? What are your personal connections with the character?

3. What would you change about the play to make the play more relevant to you and your friends today? Would you alter any of the play's language? If yes, what parts? Would you change the setting, location, time period, personality of the characters? Be creative!

4. Choose an event from *A Midsummer Night's Dream*, and connect it with your own life. Explain the event in the play, and then describe the event that occurred in your own life. How do the two events relate to each other?

FIGURE 4.7 *Sample Homework Writing Prompts*

 Getting Ready for the Big Day

Putting together a readers theater performance with high school students is chaotic and stressful. It's easy to pull out your hair trying to coordinate this kind of classroom event. We chose to put on our play in Galway's school auditorium, but it can be performed in the classroom instead, which makes things simpler. For our performance, the tutors in charge of the unit created a performance preparation checklist (see Figure 4.8) to make sure they had everything they needed to put on a successful play.

Megan and the Tutors Get a Pep Talk

Just days before the dress rehearsal, Sally called a meeting of the tutors. The kids were working hard, and we expected Sally to commend our efforts.

We couldn't have been more wrong.

"In all the years I've participated in this collaboration, I've never seen a class so unprepared as my kids are."

Astonished, I looked around at the similarly perplexed faces of my fellow tutors.

"My students don't think they're ready for a performance. They don't want to be embarrassed in front of their families and friends. This isn't looking good to me."

Performance Preparation Checklist	Yes	No
1. Does each group member have a copy of the act?		
2. Has each group turned in a list of the props and costumes those students are using?		
3. Is the auditorium reserved for the date of performance, and has its use been approved by the administration?		
4. Have you tested the microphones to make sure they are operational?		
5. Do the performers know when to arrive at the auditorium?		
6. Do the performers know where to go when they arrive at the auditorium?		
7. Do the performers know where to sit/stand while waiting their turn on stage?		
8. Are the other teachers in the school aware of the performance?		
9. Do you have a list of students from other classrooms who have permission to attend the performance?		
10. Has a tutor or teacher been designated to stand at the door to verify that entering students have permission to attend the performance?		
11. Are there signs or markers indicating where the audience should sit?		
12. If the production includes music, has the boom box, MP3 player and speakers, or stereo been set up and tested?		
13. Have you collected the MP3s, CDs, or cassette tapes from the groups and listened to them beforehand to make sure the songs are appropriate?		

FIGURE 4.8 *Performance Preparation Checklist*

Hal entered the room as we began asking Sally questions about what we were doing wrong and how we could fix it.

After Sally left, Hal tried to reassure us that we were doing a good job with the students and that we should continue preparing them for the play. He said that Sally was simply feeling anxious because the kids were starting to complain and express their fears to her.

Although we were taken aback by Sally's low confidence in us and her kids, we had seen her behave like this before in the face of her kids' nervousness. She saw herself as their guardian: a combination of mother, teacher, friend, wanting to protect them from the cruel world. *Why is Sally so scared for the kids? Does she think that if they fail, it will be the end of the world for them?* I thought to myself. "These kids are a lot tougher and smarter than people think," I told Hal.

A few minutes before class began, Hal gathered the tutors around him. "We need to raise our enthusiasm and concentrate on getting our students to be comfortable with the text. Keep doing what you've been doing and I know this will work out. It always does."

What a start to our day! If this wasn't pressure, I didn't know what was. But we walked into the classroom ready to work and challenge the students in spite of Sally's apprehension. Coaches gathered their teams in preparation for rehearsal. I walked from group to group making sure they had everything they needed, such as copies of the play, props, and costumes. (See the checklist in Figure 4.9.)

I learned that after a setback like this, it is vital for a teacher to reflect, change, and return to the classroom to begin a new day. I was beginning to see what the life of a teacher entails.

Handling Student Complaints and Fears

Whenever Shakespeare is performed, students will complain they don't understand their character or their lines. Many of them will want to switch parts or withdraw altogether.

One day, a commotion arose in one corner of the room. Ellen, one of the coaches of Team 2, was having a discussion with the school's star basketball player, Jeff, who was playing Oberon. Megan went over to see what all the fuss was about.

"Jeff doesn't want to be in the play," Ellen said. "He's afraid of being on stage, and he doesn't like the idea of using a microphone."

Although Jeff was quiet in class, everyone knew him to be confident and fearless on the basketball court. "Jeff, c'mon, we need you to play Oberon. You know the lines and you're perfect for the part," Megan told him.

"Why do I need to do this? I don't understand a word the character is saying," Jeff snapped back, his hands folded on his chest.

A Midsummer Night's Dream
Group Scene Checklist

Scene _____, Act _____

1. Is your group using any props? If so, please list them.

_____

_____

_____

2. Please list the costumes your group is using.

    Character: Description of Costume:

    _____   _____

    _____   _____

    _____   _____

    _____   _____

    _____   _____

    _____   _____

    _____   _____

    _____   _____

    _____   _____

3. Is your group changing the language of your scene in any way? If so, where is the change?

_____

_____

_____

4. Does your group need anything else to help put on your portion of the scene successfully?

_____

_____

_____

FIGURE 4.9 *Group Scene Checklist*

Thinking quickly, Megan orchestrated a demonstration. She played Oberon and asked Ellen to play Puck, Oberon's mischievous underling in the play. Megan put on a crown, Ellen grabbed a wand. Together, they modeled the scene for the whole team—reading the lines dramatically and moving around accordingly. Everyone laughed as Megan and Ellen experimented with different body movements and accents. Ellen asked the students questions about what was happening in the scene and what the lines meant. Then they passed the parts back to the students.

Perhaps seeing Ellen and Megan make fools of themselves made Jeff and his teammates feel more relaxed. Students need proof that they understand their characters and the scene. We emphasized that we weren't judging the quality of their acting but their comprehension of the play. We were there to answer their questions, help them connect with the scene, and model reading the lines. The students began to realize they had already conquered the most difficult part . . . and that acting was the fun, rewarding part.

"Say What?" Understanding the Lines

Samantha loved acting. No one in the class wanted to perform in the play more than she did. She'd been given the part of Titania in Act II, Scene 1. However, we'd forgotten that Titania's lines in that scene had all been cut. When Samantha realized her role had been eliminated, she was crestfallen. Hal immediately replaced a difficult passage in which Titania and Oberon are fighting over an Indian boy. Titania refuses to give the boy up to Oberon and makes solid arguments in defense of her possessiveness: "But she [his mother], being mortal, of that boy did die; / And for her sake I will not part with him" (2.1.135–36). She also uses arcane words and imagery:

> And on old Heims' thin and icy crown,
> An odorous chaplet of sweet summer buds
> Is, as in mockery, set.
> (2.1.109–11)

Samantha and Hal, who had agreed to play Oberon in this act, had their work cut out for them. They began by trying to understand the meaning of these lines:

> But with thy brawls thou has disturb'd our sport.
> Therefore the winds, piping to us in vain,
> As in revenge have suck'd up from the sea
> Contagious fogs.
> (2.1.87–90)

They agreed this meant that when fairies like Oberon and Titania get angry, mother nature expresses her displeasure, causing bad weather, or "contagious fogs."

Samantha was highly motivated and struggled patiently to understand and rehearse her lines. When she didn't understand what she was saying, she read the words in a sort of chant, placing a short /ă/ sound between every word, like this: "Your /ă/ buskin'd /ă/ mistress and your /ă/ warrior /ă/ love" (2.1.71).

This pattern continued for several read-throughs, but you could see her thinking, hear her begin to feel more comfortable with the difficult text. Finally, after still more practice, Samantha dropped the /ă/ sounds. She was reading with understanding, acting it out. She got it. During the performance, she had her lines memorized. She was dressed in regal red, with fairy wings, her outfit topped by a flower crown. She was a sight to see and hear. "These are the forgeries of jealousy" (2.1.81), she burst out imperiously. Repetition, combined with the desire to perform, to show her peers that she could master Shakespeare, pushed her to succeed. Also, she related to the willfulness of Titania, who did not give in to a powerful man. She loved portraying this regal and proud woman. Titania's attributes reinforced the strength of character we all knew was a part of this wonderful young lady.

Kylene Beers (2003, 204) notes, "Sounding out words a letter at a time or syllable by syllable slows a reader." She continues, "Automaticity—rapid and accurate word recognition—leads to fluency." Automaticity is exactly what Samantha achieved and all of our Galway student actors eventually achieve. Learning their parts, they go through at least two stages:

1. They study their lines closely, hardly understand them, and show little fluency.
2. Then after repetition, and discussion, something happens. They stand up, move, read their lines with animation, and make suggestions about costumes and sets. They have gained fluency and comprehension by saying the lines with meaning.

Richard Allington (2001) describes how fluency lessons have this built-in repetition and how critical these strategies are for developing comprehension and, ultimately, creating fluent readers.

■ The Dreaded Performance

The day before the performance, kids began telling coaches that certain students were deliberately going to be absent the day of the play. To get out of the performance, Galway students came up with any number of excuses.

"I have a doctor's appointment, so I won't be able to make it."

"What are you going to do? Come to my house and drag me to school? I don't want to do this."

"I'm not coming. I don't know what's going on."

We began to wonder if some of them really were going to stand us up. Megan worried she would have to change parts around to compensate for the missing students. The morning of the performance, the tutors felt a sense of relief. The past two and a half weeks had been fun but tiring for us all.

Much to our surprise, every one of our students showed up, despite their previous threats to be absent. They were nervous but excited to show off what they learned. They arrived wearing all manner of getups, lines in hand—Mike was dressed in an

elaborate African costume; Jason wore all black, his eyes hidden behind sunglasses; Alisha was dressed in overalls and wore a construction hat.

Even the tutors were in costume. They rehearsed their teams and tested the microphones as Erin, Alex, and Megan set the stage.

Sally had reserved the auditorium for two days of rehearsal, so the Galway students knew their way around the stage. The first group was positioned on stage, ready to perform. The next group of students was lined up behind the curtain on the side of the stage. The remaining two groups were in the wings, getting in a little last-minute whispered rehearsal.

Megan invited her mom to the play. She wanted her to experience the good side of Galway High School students—to see how capable these students are of achieving what many people don't think is possible. Her mom had watched Megan create the unit, design the lessons, and deal with the daily pressures of being a teacher, and now Megan wanted her to see the result, what Megan had been working so hard to accomplish.

Curtain time was fast approaching, and Megan's mom was still the only person in the auditorium. Would there be an audience? But when the bell signaled the end of the current class, students started to pour into the auditorium, and tutors escorted them to their seats. Eventually there were fifty students and three parents. We were a little disappointed at the low parent turnout but realized that many of them worked during the day and were unable to come.

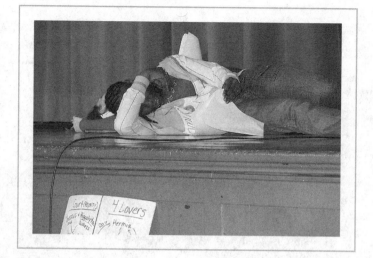

The students were a hit! The daily group work had paid off immensely; Galway students were familiar with their characters, the scenes, and the other actors. Despite their earlier nervousness, kids walked onto the stage with confidence, read their lines with enthusiasm and understanding, and interacted with humor and spontaneity. Some students didn't need their scripts; they'd practiced their lines so much they knew them by heart. The audience laughed and smiled and laughed some more.

■ Reaching the Finish Line

Moments in the play brought us to tears. Cherry, the girl who never said a word in class, turned out to be a sassy star. Mike's British accent worked perfectly with his fatherly character. Alisha, one of our most troubled students, confidently found the humor in her lines and delivered them with ease. Jeff was encouraged by the cheers coming from the crowd.

As we watched the students deliver their lines eloquently, with poise, understanding, and eagerness, we were very proud of them. Although these students had fought us all the way, they did a great job on stage. We have the video to prove it. When we looked at each other after this wonderfully successful performance, words were unnecessary. We had achieved our goals, and now the semester was over.

Like runners who experience surges of adrenaline when they cross the finish line after the last mile of a long, tiring race, we felt a rush of satisfaction when we realized our Galway kids had just read with fluency, understanding, and much joy one of the hardest texts they had ever encountered.

■ Additional Resources for Shakespeare in High School Classrooms

Plays Suitable for Classroom Performance

As You Like It

This play is also a comedy, but it is very much an ensemble work, with a marriage at the end and very strong female characters.

The Tempest

Prospero is the protagonist but not a dominating main character. This is a sweet and loving play, ripe for a classroom performance.

Much Ado About Nothing

Although this comedy has its dark moments, it is still an ensemble piece with broad slapstick humor.

Twelfth Night

This play may have one of the most bizarre plots in Shakespeare; it is convoluted and preposterous, but girls can dress as boys and boys can dress as girls, as mistaken identity rules.

Online Resources

General resources for performing Shakespeare in the classroom:

www.cln.org/themes/shakespeare.html
http://shakespeare.palomar.edu/educational.htm

Lesson plans, study guides, and electronic copies of plays:

www.folger.edu/index.cfm
www.teachersfirst.com/shakespr.shtml#
www.cummingsstudyguides.net/
www.shakespeare.com/
www-tech.mit.edu/Shakespeare/

Tips for teaching Shakespeare:

www.teach-shakespeare.com/

Shakespearean insults:

www.insults.net/html/shakespeare/
www.renfaire.com/Language/insults.html
http://members.tassie.net.au/~jaherne/bitspieces/insults.html

Multicultural and multilingual lesson plans, resources, and other materials for teaching Shakespeare:

www.angelfire.com/super2/shakespeare/index.html

MIT Shakespeare websites:

http://web.mit.edu/ensemble/www/links.html

A comprehensive guide to all things Shakespeare:

www.cummingsstudyguides.net/xShakeSph.html#top

Unfinished Business

5

The Future of America's Urban School System

▮ Falling Through the Cracks

The local paper, covering the closing of Galway High School, reported that Galway and the university never developed any unique partnerships. The efforts of our collaboration project—the advanced curricula, the academic achievements of Galway students, the positive learning experiences for all involved—were punches never felt.

Each curriculum we offered at Galway was unique, each different and dynamic, each better than the last. Each was based on what we learned the semester before; none was complete or perfect or finished. We impacted real students—at least 250 high school students passed through our classrooms. These kids performed Shakespeare, prepared writing portfolios, drafted, revised, complained, and cried at the parties at which we shared and celebrated their accomplishments.

Lots of important people—education and political leaders—knew about our collaboration project, not to mention the grant agencies that rejected our applications for funding. Even with no grant money whatsoever, the project survived for ten years without costing the school system one penny.

So how did these people contribute to our project? Did they come to us and ask us to expand it in other schools? Did people come down off the university hill to study the project, publicize it so it could be replicated, and follow up on our high school students? No. Did the city school system explore ways to expand our contribution? No. Instead, the city closed Galway High School.

Two hundred and fifty kids. Not bad, but not enough to really matter, except to the kids themselves. And what happened to those kids? Did they go to college? Did they turn their academic successes with us into lifetime achievements? Did they find new mentors? Did they know how to get help when they needed it? These questions have answers we will never know.

We wondered how these kids could come to school with so few abilities and so little self-confidence as readers and writers. But we refused to lower our expectations. And we saw the changes, the progress, the attitude adjustments, and the sense of accomplishment and appreciation expressed so warmly at each final party.

We kept thinking these kids needed more—another step, a similar project in all their subjects.

We kept thinking, what about the kids who fall through the cracks?

Revamping the System

As Megan and Hal drove home from the state middle school writing contest in May 2006, they pondered the incredible message they had just received. Megan saw it right away. The wealthy suburban school in Williamson won. Where was Galway or any city school for that matter?

Private schools like St. Benedict and suburban schools like Denville and Shady Grove have kids to represent them in this contest. So does one city school, the magnet art school, Ridgewood, but it's the exception, not the rule. These middle school kids are our future leaders—not playing sports, not playing computer games, not listening to music, but spending two days taking part in a writing contest after spending a year training to be writers.

The kids who participate in this writing contest have been taught to believe they are effective writers. They are so much more skilled as writers than our students at Galway are. And nothing we do can help the Galway students catch up.

Every year the suburban Freedom Middle School, across from the beautiful new district high school, invites our college tutors in for a Shakespeare minimarathon— they put on *A Midsummer Night's Dream* in a day. The tutors are shocked by how much more advanced these gifted and talented sixth graders are than the Galway eleventh graders, who work on the play for weeks, kicking and screaming. "Fifty times better at reading than the Galway students," one tutor lamented. "That's why I am going to work at a school like Galway," he continued. "They need me."

Kids like those who attended Galway are smart, capable, and educable. But they are also behind in a big way. And they are being educated in a very traditional setting that is as old as education itself—a school in which things are done in the same old way, the way they were done when this country was an agrarian country, eight periods a day, subject after subject. There is nothing more hopeless than doing things the same way and expecting change, to paraphrase Albert Einstein. These kids, our poor kids in this country, need a different approach. If education is the only way for these kids to get out of poverty, then education has to change.

Change, Change, Change

Is there a correlation between intelligence—the ability to think critically, for example—and one's level of reading and writing skills? Everyone who participates in this project and gets to know these disadvantaged kids discovers that the answer to this question is a resounding no. These kids think and think deeply. In a May 17, 2006, interview, Portia told us:

> I think that writing is better because a lot of times people can't talk to you or tell you what they want to say—when they write, they get it together and they write down what they want to say. You are able to understand the person more reading their writing—you're reading their mind, you're reading what they're thinking—instead of them saying it to you. A lot of times people would be ashamed of what they think and where they're coming from. So I think writing is a much better way and I think that's how we got along—'cuz everybody wrote their own things. (Bahl 2006)

Only hearing what Portia is saying, it is possible to dismiss her point. Her words have a vernacular ring; they feel like verbal drafting. However, her basic message is very smart and thoughtful: writing gives us a better understanding of our ideas and thoughts than speaking and is a little safer than speaking.

So many times, schools and teachers place kids like Portia in classes that trivialize education, that do not recognize their ability to think and reflect. Portia can strike one as loud, rude, and mean spirited. Hal first encountered her as she was walking down the hall in a group of students. He was stunned when she grabbed him and pulled him along with her. But Portia grew on us. It became clear that she was willing to do just about anything her teachers asked of her. Although she complained, she also gave excellent suggestions and more often than not would contribute interesting and insightful comments during class discussions. She was a leader in the Shakespeare unit, and her writing was interesting, varied, and stronger with each lesson. Portia is always thinking, and if a teacher builds a relationship with and truly understands her, as Sally did, that teacher will discover a bright and very optimistic young woman.

So why don't these bright kids at schools like Galway develop language skills near the level they should, and why are they so far behind so many of their rich peers in suburban schools? The potential answers include everything from environment to the time and effort it takes people with limited economic means to sustain their lives. Add to the mix a peer group hostile to formal education and schools that often treat these kids as if they had imaginary learning disabilities and we have a volatile recipe for failure.

Some researchers believe that our educational system sets urban students up for failure, particularly poor urban black students. For example, Terry Kershaw (1992) claims that standardized tests are based on the suburban curriculum, a "curriculum that few blacks have been exposed to" (160). Consequently, urban students are not academically prepared to compete with suburban students and are placed in non–college prep courses.

The late (and controversial) John Ogbu, who studied race from an anthropological perspective at the University of California, was familiar with the obstacles that African American students face in the classroom. He suggested that in order for kids from schools like Galway to be on a par with kids from upper- to middle-class, mostly white suburban schools, our entire public school system has to provide equal access to quality education. Ogbu believed that challenging, engaging curricula are missing in our urban schools, and as a result, we have denied our minority students a good education. "Minority children receiving inferior education cannot learn as much or test as well as children of the dominant group who have access to superior education," Ogbu stated (1990, 50).

Ogbu also believed language issues, cultural differences, and cultural identity prevent many African American kids from obtaining the academic status of their white peers. Ogbu and his colleague Herbert Simons wrote:

> [African American kids] know and believe that to succeed in school and to get good jobs they have to master standard English and master some white people's ways of behaving. Thus, they consider the cultural and language differences as barriers to be overcome by learning the differences. Yet they have difficulty doing so for two reasons. One is that they feel white Americans impose these differences or requirements on them. The second and more serious reason is that [African Americans] interpret the cultural and language differences as markers of collective identity to be maintained, not merely barriers to be overcome. (1998, 175)

Along these same lines, critical race theory (CRT) provides another answer to this loaded question. One of the most respected critical race theorists, Gloria Ladson-Billings, has written about why African American kids are looked down on by our society when it comes to academic issues. She writes:

> CRT raises questions about its [curriculum in urban schools] quality. Many children of the dominant group [white suburban kids] have an opportunity for "enriched" and "rigorous" curriculum. Poor [children], immigrant [children], bilingual [children], and children of color usually are confined to the "basics." (2004, 59)

It's no wonder suburban kids have the high test scores, while the urban schools continue to fail and be deemed in a state of academic emergency.

Etta R. Hollins, another critical race theorist, writes about how teachers can make their curriculum more successful for kids in urban schools. Hollins believes the most powerful teachers she sees in urban education are those who connect curriculum to the social and cultural backgrounds of their students (Ladson-Billings 1999, 217–18). Holding high expectations and teaching meaningful lessons connected to the lives of their students are two important ways teachers can change our public school system into a system that offers equitable education for all students.

CURRICULUM

The reason most school systems still employ tracking is that many administrators, teachers, parents, and students feel that not every student can be successful in an advanced curriculum. (However, at Galway, the kids who weren't supposed to be able to do the advanced curriculum did it.) Students not in an advanced curriculum—students of color, immigrants, the rural and urban poor, and children whose native language is not English—are sentenced to the "pedagogy of poverty," or endless drills, worksheets, and remedial instruction that will guarantee a lifelong hatred for learning (Haberman 1991). According to Haberman, the pedagogy of poverty consists of:

- giving information
- asking questions
- giving directions
- making assignments
- monitoring seatwork
- reviewing assignments
- giving tests
- reviewing tests
- assigning homework
- reviewing homework
- settling disputes
- punishing noncompliance
- marking papers
- giving grades

Haberman admits these tasks are inevitable for teachers but are ineffective if "taken together and performed to the systematic exclusion of other acts" (1991, 290), and he believes that this pedagogy has become the signature of poverty-bound education.

What teachers and schools need to do more of, he suggests, is teach student-centered pedagogy.

Ladson-Billings (2004, 59–60) interprets student-centered pedagogy as:

- involving students with issues important to their lives
- explaining human differences
- teaching students about major concepts and ideas
- helping students plan their future
- asking students to apply ideas to their world
- mixing students into heterogeneous groups
- questioning common sense
- helping students redo, polish, and perfect their work
- asking students to reflect on their own lives
- accessing technology in meaningful ways

In an advanced, meaningful, and student-centered curriculum, teachers and students have high expectations.

In our urban school project, we implement an advanced curriculum that we feel satisfies Haberman's and Ladson-Billings' definitions of effective teaching.

- We use classroom materials that promote higher-level thinking.
- We connect our lessons to the lives of students.
- We assign projects that encourage discovery of knowledge.
- We use workshops to personalize instruction.
- We encourage social interaction between teacher and students.
- We model how to work in groups.
- We learn for a purpose.
- We assemble student portfolios that demonstrate growth.
- We train enthusiastic, passionate teachers who build bridges between the curriculum and the students.
- We maintain a balance between teacher instruction and student application.
- We share student work.
- We celebrate student work.
- We create a comfortable classroom environment so students feel open to discussing their ideas.
- We give students the freedom to make mistakes.

How do we set high expectations in our classroom?

- We get to know students.
- We expect students to be able to do the work because they can.
- We encourage students to be confident in their abilities.

- We encourage students to take pride in their work.
- We don't place limitations on students.
- We don't accept poor effort.
- We don't let students give up on themselves.
- We give students a chance to redo their work.
- We praise students for real achievements.

Ladson-Billings and Haberman have studied urban classrooms, and their research helps us understand what is effective with urban students. If urban teachers know the characteristics of an effective, advanced curriculum and know what it takes to be a successful urban teacher (as outlined above), then they can adjust their curriculum and pedagogy to create more successful learning experiences for their students. Ultimately, the teachers in urban schools have the power to change our educational system.

TEACHERS

Linda Darling-Hammond (2000, 266), professor and expert on teacher education, sees four problems that teachers of African Americans face in their classrooms.

1. Schools that serve large numbers of African American students are least likely to offer the kind of curriculum and teaching needed to meet high academic standards.
2. Many urban systems have focused their curricula more on learning basic skills by rote than on thoughtfully examining literature and writing often and at length.
3. The lack of equal access to challenging and high-quality materials is a serious impediment to progress.
4. Practices associated with higher reading scores—using trade books and literature rather than basal readers and workbooks, encouraging discussions and group projects, having students make presentations—are less likely to be made available to urban and minority students.

C. Talbert-Johnson (2004, 29–30) identifies six characteristics that define culturally responsive teachers, which we believe are solutions teachers of impoverished, at-risk students can bring to the problems Darling-Hammond sees in our schools. Culturally responsive teachers:

1. are socially conscious, that is, they recognize that there are many ways of perceiving reality and that these ways are influenced by one's location in the social order
2. have affirming views of students from diverse backgrounds, recognizing resources for learning in all students

3. see themselves as both responsible for and capable of bringing about educational change that will make a difference in the lives of all students
4. understand how learners construct knowledge and are capable of promoting learners' knowledge construction
5. know about the lives of their students
6. use their knowledge about students' lives to design instruction that builds on students' prior knowledge in new contexts (while stretching them beyond the familiar)

In our Galway project, Sally was our culturally responsive model for the student teachers learning how to become urban English teachers of at-risk kids. This is the reason Sally started the project. She gave student teachers a chance to step out of their theoretical education classes and into the real world where they would encounter all the aspects of teaching: lesson preparation, teaching techniques, teacher-student relationships, and classroom management. Our student teachers faced the negatives about being a teacher of at-risk students:

- intimidating-looking students
- lessons planned for fifty minutes that end up taking fifteen
- enthusiasm for teaching smashed by apathetic students
- constant interruptions such as fire alarms and PA announcements
- strange kids who walk into classes for no reason
- angry custodians upset about having to unlock classrooms to retrieve missing microphones
- cafeteria workers resentful about lost parking places
- kids mouthing off during class
- endless computer and printer problems

But there were also hard-won positives:

- scary kids who became allies and friends over time
- kids who took pride in their work and gained a sense of hope in themselves
- student-centered lessons in which kids wrote, read, and performed
- the end-of-the-year celebration of mutual respect and accomplishments: the Galway kids realized what they were capable of learning, and the student teachers realized the truth about city kids and city schools

Lisa Alston, a Galway project alumna, now teaches with Sally in another urban high school. Lisa, raised in a wealthy suburb and a product of suburban schools, realized not only that she could teach in the city but also that it was her destiny.

Patty Aimes, another alumna, now teaches in the suburbs. When her students reveal their stereotypical idea of city students, Patty corrects them with stories about

Mike and Emily and Johnny, kids she met in the project. Patty brings home the reality of city life to these suburban kids.

How's that for teacher training?

Sally's hope was to help create teachers like Lisa and Patty. And during the ten years of the project, she has seen many aspiring teachers overcome the stereotypes of urban schools and kids. Our Galway project, if replicated in more colleges of education and urban schools, could help city teachers, rural teachers, and suburban teachers gain respect and a realistic understanding of at-risk kids and their classrooms.

COMMUNITY

"Get help," Sally tells all of the student teachers when she talks to them about urban high school teaching. And here is where things really do need to change, not only in the specific approach to curricula but also in the hearts and minds of the community. We can't help but feel that schools like Galway have been abandoned and the kids we taught there are, to many Americans, forgotten and don't count. Either this changes or Megan's generation also leaves behind an undereducated population of poor kids. But it will be even worse because jobs that do not require college education will be scarce.

Schools like Galway need two layers of volunteer support to ensure the successful education of our most fragile students. The people in the community make up the first layer—people working in corporations, law firms, hospitals, small businesses, who are from similar ethnic and cultural backgrounds as the students and who serve as role models. Preservice teachers from colleges of education working with students in the classroom make up the second layer. Both types of volunteers must tutor, offer counsel, serve as mentors, help scaffold instruction, and encourage kids to become confident in an academic environment.

Megan Ruminates on Affecting Eternity

In his office, hidden among the piles of books, Hal has a framed quotation: above a yellowish-green abstract image resembling a butterfly are the words, "A teacher affects eternity. He can never tell when his influence stops." I used to stare at it when I had trouble writing or when I was deep in thought.

I have always believed that teachers are rewarded nicely for their work—summers off, long holiday breaks, great retirement plans, and excellent health benefits. But it was not until I became a teacher that I realized that the ultimate reward is that we have the power to change students' lives for the better. As the image in Hal's framed quotation suggests, teachers can have a "butterfly effect" on their students. One little thing they do, say, or teach in the classroom, good or bad, can impact a student and change the course of his or her life forever.

As an aspiring teacher, I dream of impacting my students and motivating them to be the best people they can be, but I never would have imagined that I would get the chance to do this in my first teaching experience at Galway High School.

Mike was the kind of student who often goes unseen and unheard in the classroom; he did his work, kept to himself, and was careful not to attract attention from his peers or teachers. He was too shy to raise his hand or volunteer answers. On the first day of class, I sat down next to Mike and introduced myself. Immediately, I noticed Mike's bright smile; kind, dark brown eyes; and his slight African accent. Since I had never been to Africa but have always wanted to go there someday, I asked him about his home country. When I asked Mike about how he felt about writing, he said that English had always been one of his favorite classes in school. He also said, "I'd really like to go to law school someday."

During the first week of class, the tutors and high school students wrote autobiographies to get to know one another. I walked around the room helping students, stopping at Mike's desk from time to time. While most of the kids had barely a paragraph written, Mike had a full page. His handwriting was neat and his paragraphs organized. After reading his rough draft, I told him I liked his writing, and his face instantly lit up. "Really? Nah. It's not that good." Pointing out good sentences he'd written, the vivid imagery he'd included in his writing, and his structured paragraphs, I assured Mike he had a talent in writing. "See, Mike, you are a good writer. I think you have a hidden gift," I told him, and we laughed together. Mike became excited about his writing, and each day I watched as he put more and more effort into his work. For the first time, I realized how much positive feedback can boost a student's self-confidence.

Throughout the semester, I continued to talk to Mike about his writing and about his going to college. Since he had been in the United States for only one year, it was hard for Mike to conceive that he would ever go to college. He was unfamiliar with the admissions process and knew very little about the colleges nearby. I brought him a promotional video put out by my university, which gave him information on the majors available. Since he was interested in playing college soccer, I also gave him the men's soccer team game schedule and the head coach's email address.

One Saturday during the semester, when Mike was walking around downtown with a few of his friends, he was jumped by two boys from Galway's rival school, Dublin. The Dublin students mistook Mike for another student but realized it too late to stop beating him up. Mike was put in the hospital for a weekend. Welcome to the United States.

When Mike returned to school, I cried when I saw the stitches, bruises, and swollen lip. "I'm so sorry that this happened to you, Mike. Are you okay? Do you need anything?" I asked him as I gave him the candy I'd bought especially for him. I could not understand why anyone would want to hurt this sweet, reserved boy. I was angry that kids could be so mean.

Despite that painful incident, Mike was determined to improve his writing skills and work hard in school. As Mike and I continued to work together, he began to open up to me and to his classmates. He became more outgoing and was one of the stars in our Shakespeare performance. He looked happy.

At the class celebration of the end of our semester, Mike gave me a handwritten card and a big hug. "I still don't know what I'm going to do about college, but I'll keep in touch. Thank you for your encouragement," he told me. Not knowing what he was going to do with his life or who was going to take my place and encourage him, I was sad to see him leave. Yet somehow I knew that I would see or hear from Mike again.

One summer night, hanging out with my brother, I heard my cell phone ring. I didn't recognize the number that came up on caller ID, so I let it go through to voice-mail. "Hi, Megan, this is Mike from Galway. I just wondered how your summer is going, and I wanted to tell you that I got into York State University! I'm so excited! My mom is so proud of me. They don't have a soccer team, but I'm going to play intramurals. Call me back whenever you can. Thank you again, Megan, for everything you did for me at Galway. God bless you always." I was touched by his message, tearing up a little as I realized the butterfly effect I'd had. It had taken so little to make him realize that he was a good writer—a few encouraging words and some extra attention. I had a big smile on my face for the rest of the night.

The following afternoon, I called Mike. He sounded thrilled about going to college; he couldn't wait for his orientation so that he could sign up for his classes and meet his dorm roommate.

"I'm so happy for you, Mike! You better keep me updated," I giggled. "I know it's a little early, but do you know what you want to study in college?"

"You'll never guess! I'm going to become an English major, Megan! You made me see how much I love writing."

I felt like I had won the lottery! Not only was Mike going to college, but he finally recognized his writing abilities. I thought to myself, *What a reward for being a teacher! It can't get any better than this.*

And yet. . . .

Being an English major in college, I know what Mike is about to face. He will meet arrogant English professors who will make him read huge amounts of literature, vastly removed from anything he has ever read or experienced. He will be sitting next to English majors who went to excellent high schools with challenging English curricula. He may become alienated or find it difficult to connect with his classmates. He might have to cope with grades that will discourage him and unsupportive comments on papers. It is unlikely that he will meet classmates from Africa.

I know that if I had another year working with Mike, if I were assigned to be his mentor, I could help him overcome the academic obstacles and the alienation that every student faces when entering college. Another year with Mike would help him prepare to handle the challenges in a rigorous college English program. Maybe he will get through college without my help . . . but I'm still worried.

Mike taught me that we can't just abandon these kids after they graduate. That's why Hal and I recommend that volunteers and education students provide a follow-up year of personal aid and attention.

FOLLOW-UP TUTORS

Portia graduated from a different high school this spring, and Hal still sees her. She's a checker at his supermarket, and while she rings up his groceries, she and Hal discuss the possibility of her attending the local university. She lacks her natural ebullience when at work, and it's easy to tell she doesn't want to spend the rest of her life in a supermarket. Hal has given Portia his email address and offered to help her with the basics of admission and financial aid. So far she has not taken him up on it.

Hal has had better luck with Samantha, who also graduated. Samantha spent a day with Hal at the university attending and participating in college classes. Afterward, Hal took Samantha to the admissions office, where she picked up in person information that had been sent to the wrong address. (Samantha moves a lot.) And she went to the financial aid office and was given instructions on what to do next.

Many of our Galway students, students like Mike, Portia, and Samantha, go to college, some with loans and some with grants. Where do they end up? Many are relegated to developmental programs in open admissions universities where they pay for remedial courses that do not count for graduation. The potential for failure is great, and there is a good chance these students will never complete college. They will have lost time, resources, and worst of all, hope. Even if students like Mike get into a regular college track, they may find themselves in need of support services such as tutoring or just someone who can help with the basic first-year issues of university life. His more wealthy counterparts will have many of these peer support systems in place, but it is unlikely that Mike will find many students with similar backgrounds. If we can help him during a follow-up year of mentoring, he may be able to make a smoother transition into college.

We have been thinking about this program since we started the Galway project. It wouldn't take much, and it would make an enormous difference, but we don't have the resources. We know it's the right thing to do, and we know how much Galway students going to college need it. Occasionally it happens informally between a college mentor and a graduating high school senior.

Our proposal to monitor our at-risk urban students during their first year in college is centered around follow-up tutor-mentors who will help them:

- deal with dorm and social life
- adjust to college academics
- schedule classes
- plan for the future (majors, networking, careers)

This follow-up program requires few resources other than those that are already in place: volunteers from the business community, alumni from the high schools, student teachers, preteacher candidates. Of course, one can give thousands of excuses why this kind of mentorship can't be done:

"It's too much work."

"Community leaders have no time for this."

"Education students have their own problems, their own demands on their time."

"Universities aren't set up to do this kind of work."

Yet with a little flexibility and some out-of-the-box thinking, an urban high school teacher can design a follow-up mentoring program that benefits the students, the school, and the community.

Who Pays?

How many times have we heard, "You can't just throw money at a problem"? It's the baby boomers' mantra to protect their own interests and allow them to abandon the larger community without feeling guilty. In Galway's district, the community voted against a levy to support the school when it was clear the physical plant was in serious disrepair and it was almost impossible to find a working printer there. How it could get worse is hard to imagine . . . but it will. The price for fixing all of this is very high: the National Education Association places the price tag for necessary school capital improvements nationwide at $322 billion (Baines and Foster 2006, 224). Things are fine in Forest Hills, however, where homes cost upward of a million dollars. Just recently, this school district built a sleek, beautiful new public high school with incredible facilities and technological resources. The architecture of this school is so luxurious that it is an edifying experience simply to be in the building.

We have two Americas here: one rich, one poor; one on the path to great comfort, opportunity, and wealth, one struggling to make ends meet without much hope of a future. Jonathon Kozol gets this right in *Savage Inequalities* (1991), where he provides heartbreaking evidence of the economic advantages rich kids have over poor kids in schooling.

Our Galway project cost the school district, its students, and the community nothing. But to fix schools like Galway in a way that matches Forest Hills is going to cost a lot of money. The alternative, however, is to perpetuate a poor underclass without marketable skills. Throwing money into the school is not enough; that's why we wrote this book—we want to show where schools need to change. However, schools like Galway will continue to fail if their communities refuse to or cannot support them. Community support has to include giving money to build facilities like Forest Hills and providing staff and materials. So who pays?

GRANTS

Once we realized Galway High School was under threat of closure, we looked for ways to communicate what we were doing since we felt the project had the potential to help improve the quality of at-risk urban education. Our first attempt at replication was to apply for grants. We spent a year educating ourselves on how to write grants, then applied for three. The process was frustrating and antithetical to the nature of the Galway project. It became very clear that we could easily spend more time writing grant proposals than working with urban students in the classroom. Also, so much of what the grant agencies asked for was not answerable until we had the resources we were seeking. How could we give the specific, quantifiable evaluations the grant requests required without an army of psychometricians? We kept thinking, *There is no one available to do the grant work. It's just us. How can we do what we are required to do?* Going the grant route seemed to require professional grant writers, outside evaluators, psychometricians, and office staff who could identify and help us apply for appropriate grants—but we could not afford this kind of help.

A paradox: in order to be awarded grant money, we had to spend money we didn't have. Urban school successes, we are convinced, are more like our project, "mom-and-pop stores" created by imaginative and courageous teachers like Sally. Based on our experiences, normal grant providers don't support the kinds of innovations necessary to turn urban public schools around. They are too conventional, concerned with formal evaluations that in reality have the potential to shape classrooms in the *wrong* direction. Grants we applied for were too prescriptive. As long as grants require an enormous amount of formality, extreme specificity, and abundant administrative resources, urban education innovations will for the most part remain unfunded and unknown and will receive a death sentence when the creative teacher leaves the classroom.

The John D. and Catherine T. MacArthur Foundation does it differently. They find you. You cannot apply to be a MacArthur Fellow; rather, the Foundation finds the recipients through appointed nominators. Potential MacArthur Fellows aren't even aware they are being considered until they receive the phone call telling them they've been chosen. Why can't urban education grants look more like that? The benefits would be enormous. These grants would:

- reward low-profile, innovative classroom teachers who do not have the time or resources to spend preparing grant applications—the people who most likely are creating the solutions that could save urban schools
- uncover the finest experimental urban education programs already in place
- help replicate out-of-the-box thinking in urban schools, which are often stuck in bureaucratic red tape and city politics
- allow teachers who are creative to spread their ideas to other teachers and schools

Here's how it might work.

1. Nominators seek out innovative classrooms and programs.
2. Grant agencies send on-site teams to investigate the quality and creativity of these classrooms and programs.
3. Grants are given to teachers to help them develop materials to share with other schools.
4. Grant-awarded classrooms are designated as "special sites" for educators to visit, study, and replicate.
5. Evaluation teams study these special sites to determine their effectiveness.
6. Schools and teachers who replicate these special sites are given financial and logistical support.
7. Communication systems—websites, webcasts, newsletters, and research bulletins—are developed and funded to increase the number of these sites.

This approach is just one of many possible ways to improve urban schools. The essential point we're making here is that there needs to be a new approach to grant-giving that allows teachers to experiment with urban teaching methods, not take time and effort away from their classroom to write grant applications.

PHILANTHROPY

Financing our educational system is one of the biggest conundrums of our time, and the one thing we know is that it isn't working—unless by *working* one means the current inequitable system in which some schools thrive and other schools wither. Galway High School was rapidly deteriorating—missing ceiling tiles exposed the building's infrastructure, the computers were outdated and malfunctioning. And there are schools in worse shape than Galway. One day, we visited another school, and Megan was shocked. She had never seen an uglier, dingier, darker school.

School funding is one of the major challenges of our nation. How can we fix a couple of generations' worth of failing urban school systems? Certainly some of the more generous and visionary philanthropists are working on it. For instance, on June 26, 2006, Warren E. Buffett, the Nebraskan investment genius, donated 85 percent of his fortune to the Bill and Melinda Gates Foundation. Gates has spent billions of dollars aiding American urban public education.

But is philanthropy enough to solve the ubiquitous problems of at-risk education, or is it simply an excuse taxpayers use to get out of the educational game? All the philanthropic foundations combined cannot realistically assume the responsibility of the American citizenry to ensure a future for the young and vulnerable generations that succeed them. Since 1994, eighteen of the wealthiest families in America, including the Waltons of Wal-Mart and the Mars family of the candy fortune, have spent $500 million lobbying for estate tax repeal (Johnston 2006). These people give very little of the fortunes they have amassed to charity. People like Gates and Buffett are rare, generous, civic-minded billionaires, but no matter how much money they have, they cannot provide a quality education for every American child.

■ Final Reflections

We have no definitive answers for solving the school-funding problem. Who does? So we are left with questions. We will leave you with questions as well, questions related to all the issues we have raised in this chapter. We hope you think about these questions, discuss your ideas, and start on the long and very difficult path of educating the kids of our nation's Galway High Schools.

1. Does your curriculum meet the criteria of an advanced curriculum?
2. If not, what are some ways you can transform your curriculum into an advanced curriculum?
3. How does your curriculum serve students? What would you keep and what would you eliminate from your curriculum to make it more advanced, interactive, and student centered?
4. How would you rate yourself as a culturally responsive teacher (see Figure 5.1)? How does your curriculum reflect your attitude and behavior? (Provide specific evidence.)
5. Who do you consider to be good role models in your community? How can you get them to help your school?
6. How can you use your local university and area colleges to help your school?
7. How will you help train volunteers and preservice teachers?
8. Do you follow up on your students after they graduate from your school? If so, how? And if not, why not?
9. How can you use your volunteers to help students following their graduation?
10. Do you have any funding ideas?

	Never	Rarely	Sometimes	Frequently	Constantly	Evidence
Do you recognize that there are many ways one may perceive reality and that these ways are influenced by one's location in the social order?						
Do you hold affirming views of students from diverse backgrounds, recognizing different ways that students learn?						
Do you see yourself as both responsible for and capable of bringing about educational change that will make a difference in the lives of all students?						
Do you understand how learners construct knowledge and that you are capable of promoting learners' knowledge construction?						
Do you take time to get to know about the lives of your students?						
Do you use your knowledge about students' lives to design instruction that builds on their prior knowledge in new contexts (while stretching them beyond the familiar)?						

FIGURE 5.1 *Rating Worksheet on the Characteristics of a Culturally Responsive Teacher*

Changing Times,
Changing Lives

Insanity is doing the same thing over and over and expecting different results.
—Albert Einstein

Our Iceberg Is Melting
—John Kotter and Holger Rathgeber

Life changes.

Megan has moved on. She completed student teaching with the highest rating possible. Last Saturday I attended Megan's wedding. And she has accepted a teaching job out of state. Yet I consider Megan at risk. I do not know where she will be teaching, and I certainly have no idea how she will be mentored as a new teacher. Megan has enormous talent. Will this school have the structures in place and the staff to guide Megan through the perilous stage of being a novice teacher? Will Megan survive the early years to go on to fulfill her potential as an outstanding teacher/educator? "Our schools are like a bucket with a hole in the bottom, and we keep pouring in teachers," claims Thomas G. Carroll, the president of the National Commission on Teaching and America's Future. The commission reports that "nearly a third of all new teachers leave the profession after just three years, and that after five years almost half are gone—a higher turnover rate than the past" (Dillon 2007, A13).

The project has also moved on and, happily, continues. One of the unique features of Galway was how close it was to the university; my students could walk over without missing classes. When Galway closed, I didn't see how the project could survive. However, Sally moved to a school ten miles away, and we gave it a shot. Could my students get there? They did, without problems. Fortunately, our new school also has plenty of parking. A laboratory classroom remains accessible.

This new school is every bit as urban as Galway, although it has a different mix. The school is also physically much older, and if you stopped to consider your surroundings when inside, it could sap your spirits. Naturally, the only computers are ancient, and the school has none of the amenities of the rich suburban schools. In all fairness to the school district and the state, there are efforts under way to build new urban schools. (That's the reason given for closing Galway, to cut expenses in order to finance the new buildings.)

Our curriculum, within its basic structure, remains fluid, as always; lots of writing, a dynamic reading workshop, a Shakespeare performance, and an end-of-semester celebration. The changes are most evident in the reading workshop. This semester we worked short stories into the workshop, and the result was dynamite. Our student teachers made strong connections to the stories; had the high school students reading in class; created intellectually challenging, powerful writing assignments; and held discussions based on the themes of the short stories. It was one of the project's best reading workshops, although the tutors selected the stories, not the students. I want the high schoolers to continue to have a say in at least some of their reading, but I have to admit, for the most part, our high school students were motivated and worked hard even though the stories were assigned.

One issue that always separates our at-risk high school students from advanced classes is homework. We have never been able to get these students to complete work outside the classroom with any consistency, and that is still true. Whatever the reasons—complex home lives, lack of structure and motivation—they don't do homework.

This week we are preparing the showcase portfolios. Next week is spring break, and my student teachers will go back to the university campus to prepare for the Shakespeare unit and the end-of-semester party.

My college students from last semester who visited the high school class we are currently teaching told me that these kids were going to "kill us," that this was a "very wicked" class. They were wrong. This current class is the best I've experienced. These students really like having us with them. We will see how the Shakespeare goes. The beginning of the Shakespeare unit is always tough.

Sally will continue to teach for one more year (and perhaps longer), so if all goes well, the project has at least another year. After that, Sally's replacement may take over. I plan on staying for five more years, and I will continue the project for as long as I am invited. I cannot imagine my professional life without this direct experience in the trenches. I am in an urban school classroom with at-risk high school kids at least three days a week. I have seen things accomplished that I never thought possible, and I now have renewed hope that when Megan's generation of teachers retires, more of this country's "unseen" kids will be getting the education they need, one that will make a huge difference in their lives.

Hal Foster

Afterword

When I first walked into a classroom as a teacher I felt very much alone. All of them, and just one of me. Hundreds of them, in ranks, like a phalanx of Caesar's army, lined up there facing me, staring, unsmiling, unblinking, sizing me up, judging my resilience, my reflexes, my speed, my strength, my tolerance for pain, abuse, and the chewing of gum in my classroom. Their classroom.

Well, perhaps not hundreds—thirty, I suppose—but they looked like hundreds. I vividly remember them as hundreds. Hundreds forged into one team, a troop, a battalion, a brigade, hardened by years in classrooms like this one dealing with interlopers like me. They'd undergone basic training in kindergarten and fought together as a unit ever since, side by side, honing their tactics, sharpening their coordination, perfecting their maneuvers, driving substitute after substitute into selling insurance and teacher after teacher into bar-tending. Even the most courageous principal and the boldest of assistant-principals had retreated before them into the relative safety of their offices where they could write memos to teachers and search Monster.com for quieter employment in law-enforcement, firefighting, and drug interdiction.

I had marched into that room with roughly forty days of student teaching, a cheap suit, and a bad haircut; they had, I calculated, a total of 54,000 man/woman days of experience (minus a few for colds and unexcused absences). I was outnumbered, outgunned, outmatched, and I knew it. They were tenth graders and they were terrifying.

And, I'm ashamed to admit, they all looked like me.

I was in the same school I'd attended as a student, so these were students out of the same community I'd lived in, and it hadn't changed much in the five years since I'd left. That meant that they were mostly middle class, mostly white, mostly, well, just like me. And still I quaked. I wonder what it would have been like if I'd found my first job in a different school, perhaps one more like Galway, with students not quite so middle class, not quite so comfortable and complacent, not quite so "seen" as I was. If these students, my mirror images, the ones I'd *seen* all my school life, were so frightening, how might I have reacted to the *unseen* students Hal and Megan and their education students met at Galway. I'd rather not speculate about it. . . .

Back to that first day. Community was the last thing on my mind. I didn't seem to have one. There was no one to back me up, no one to cover my flank. I was alone. All I could do was keep my back to the blackboard, my chalk sharpened, and the path to the door unobstructed. Survival was the issue.

Gradually, however, my fear began to subside. After a year or two I mustered the courage to turn my back on them and write something on the board. Nothing more than a fragment at first—I didn't have the courage for a complete sentence—but even a fragment was a start. By the time I had progressed, one small, timid step at a time, to writing full sentences, even an occasional paragraph or two, I had learned that they weren't all that hostile and dangerous, and that I had a fair-to-middling chance of surviving less guarded encounters with them. In time, I began to suspect that these students were much like real people. They might even have, I speculated, lives of their own, fears and hopes of their own, dreams and doubts like those of the real people I knew outside the classroom. If I could come to *see* them that way, see their fears and hopes, who knows what might result.

Ultimately, I came to realize that they *were*, in fact, real people. A small epiphany, but significant, nonetheless. I came to see them, and to see that they weren't just a phalanx, just a force aligned against me. They were a collection of diverse, unique, often fascinating individuals. Some were much like me; some were different. Some had encountered very little of the world; some more than I would ever want to confront, myself. Some would even become friends. But all of them wanted to be seen, to be heard, to be respected, to be taught, and to be part of a community. Gradually, much too gradually and slowly, we began to form a community.

I suspect that Hal and Megan learned that much faster than I did. They write about the community that they joined and helped shape in the school they worked in, an inner-city school with some problems but with rich resources in its students, those students too easily left *unseen*. If their book does nothing more, it will serve us well simply by its vivid reminder that a school is a small society, a community of learners who come together to try to make sense of their lives, to talk and write about the human experience, to learn what they need to know in order to make their way through the world and to make the most of the short time they have in it. And they remind us that all of our students, even those who hide in the shadows or have been forced into the dark corners of our system, deserve to be part of that community.

Their story of the evolving community in Galway denies us the possibility of thinking of the school as a factory, a production line to generate some successful test-takers and relegate the others to menial work, to sort our students into those who run the corporations and reap the profits and those who will be sent off to fight and die defending, extending, and enriching those corporations. Hal and Megan portray the school—one school in this case, but potentially many, most, perhaps all—as a place where people might come together not to be sorted into winners and losers, not to compete and contest and conquer, but to talk and think and learn, and in the process to come to accept, respect, perhaps even value, one another. And in the process develop a community with respect and opportunity for all of our children.

School is perhaps a microcosm of society and as such it surely imitates the society of which it is a part. But it might also shape that society. It might become the model that the broader society would do well to imitate. Hal and Megan tell us in this story that the schools don't have to replicate for our students the isolation, violence, predation, and indifference to the individual—especially the poorer, less privileged individual—that we find elsewhere. Rather, they might be humane, respectful, cooperative, and nurturing, dedicated to eliciting the best from all of our children, to seeing and hearing all of them, to giving them a voice, to deepening the bonds between them and strengthening the community that they constitute.

There is no reason—no excuse—for anyone to see the classroom as the frightening, hostile terrain it was for me on that first day of teaching. I should have walked in expecting to find, and finding, a community eager to learn, welcoming to newcomers, respectful of our differences, committed to achieving the best for all. Perhaps if I'd read *America's Unseen Kids* before that first day, and learned what it teaches me, I wouldn't have seen that classroom as them-against-me, but as us, all of us, in it together. Perhaps the book will teach many of us not to view the children we meet in our classrooms, whoever they may be, as "them," as "those children," but as "us," "our children."

We really are in it together, as *America's Unseen Kids* tells us. We are all part of this classroom, this school, this community, this society, this country, this world. Perhaps if we begin to work and think and collaborate as Hal and Megan suggest, we may have a better chance of holding it all together in these difficult times.

Robert E. Probst
Florida International University

Acknowledgments

It takes a lot of courage to release the familiar and seemingly secure,
to embrace the new. But there is no real security in what is no longer
meaningful. There is more security in the adventurous and exciting,
for in movement there is life, and in change there is power.

—Alan Cohen

Many of the Galway and university students agreed to help with this book, and we are indebted to them all. We thank them for their participation, cooperation, and hard work. We would like to give special thanks to these students in particular for helping us in myriad ways: William Chad Bever, Angel Foster, Brooke Hinson, Eric Howell, Erika Hughett, Danny Johnson, Quanita Mendoza, Maureen Miller, Joe Miller, Darnell Monroe, Susanne Nachampasak, David Parks III, Sarah Petry, Brianne Polk, Markese Reaves, Angela Reese, Marcedes Sanders, Marlene Sell, Rachel Shelby, Tonie Spirtos, David Staley, and Catherine Stoynoff.

Of course, we could not have written this book without Sally. Not only did she let the student teachers get to know her students and experiment with lessons, but she also gave us the freedom to write about her and her urban teaching methods.

We also thank the university for giving us the support and resources that made this book possible. We thank our provost, Beth Stroble, our deans, Pat Nelson and Cynthia Capers, our assistant dean, Evonn Welton, our department chair, Bridgie Ford, our associate dean, Sajit Zachariah, and our administrative assistants, Susan Wheeler (who helped every step of the way) and Cheryl Collins.

We are very indebted to Raymond J. McGowan, attorney at law, who provided us with legal advice and developed our consent forms.

We were also fortunate to have expert advice. Art Palacas, linguist and friend, shared his insights about language with us, which we used throughout this book. Francis Broadway, professor of science education, offered us sage advice about viewing the racial issues we encountered throughout the project. Russell D. Sibert offered us his time and expertise.

Naomi Silverman, of Lawrence Erlbaum Associates, made us realize that we really could write a book on this subject. An outstanding editor, she helped guide the beginnings of *America's Unseen Kids*. We are grateful for her initial support and advice.

Also, we feel so fortunate to have the guidance of Lisa Luedeke, our editor at Heinemann. Her advice has been outstanding. Offered with kindness, it has made this book better at every turn. Thank you, Lisa.

Alan Huisman showed incomparable skill as he edited our book in preparation for production. We owe Alan much thanks for his careful and thorough reading.

And finally, we are grateful to the excellent and professional production and editorial staff, including Vicki Kasabian, Stephanie Colado, Kim Arney, Chrysta Meadowbrooke, Diane Freed, and Susan Hernandez.

▣ Hal's Acknowledgments

I wrote this book as my farewell to the Galway project. Galway High School was closing, and I needed to close this important chapter of my life as well. But the project did not die after all. Sally transferred to another city high school. The ten-minute ride made it just close enough. The principal of the new school also transferred from Galway. She understood the project and gave us full permission to continue. Better yet, Sally suggested that one of the other English teachers who transferred from Galway could sponsor the project after Sally retired. This teacher, a student in an early Galway project, is the perfect person to take over. As for my replacement when I retire . . . that remains an unknown.

Megan Nosol came at the right time, with the right set of skills. Our slow but steady ability to work and write with each other is another story that I would like to tell someday. Megan is newly everything—newly licensed, newly married. For me, Megan was always about the next forty years, fixing a broken system, which my generation had failed to do. Megan is the voice of the new generation of teachers and educators. Megan is the voice of hope in this book.

Megan's ability to grow into the role of peer writer and collaborator is a testament to her maturity and her skills, primarily her ability to learn and adapt. I tell everyone that without Megan there would be no book because this started as a student project designed for her, my graduate assistant. I needed a push to take on a project of this size and complexity, and Megan gave me one. This is not my first book, but I wondered whether I was up to it; amazingly, young Megan Nosol, starting out in education, was very much up to it. I am fortunate to have her as my coauthor.

Kylene Beers has been an inspiration to me for many years, and without her support and professional example this book would not have happened. Most of Megan's and my writing days included perusing a well-worn copy of Kylene's phenomenal book, *When Kids Can't Read: What Teachers Can Do*. Kylene remains one of my most valuable friends. I am very fortunate to have her support. My respect and admiration for Kylene is limitless.

The other book that we constantly pored over while we wrote is the second edition of *Response and Analysis: Teaching Literature in Secondary Schools*. Bob Probst has been my intellectual hero for many years. He has done more for the teaching of literature than anyone I know. Our Galway curriculum is dedicated to his influence and ideas.

Amanda Badar was my graduate assistant during my grant-writing phase. Mandy was instrumental in the design of the curriculum that we describe in this book, and I am indebted to her on many levels, including the friendship that we maintain.

Sharon Greenblatt, now an English teacher, is one of the only people involved in the project besides Megan and me whom I mention in the chapters by her real name. She helped me in so many ways, always willing to share stories or fill in the holes in my memory. If Sharon is our future, then our future looks good.

Lois Stover, one of the smartest persons I have ever known, gives me advice that is always helpful and accurate. Her support of this project and book have made it possible for me to continue on the path that led both to be successful.

Lawrence Baines has been a supporter and friend for years. He has visited Galway, and his support and advice have been invaluable assets for me as I complete this project.

Amanda Smith, a former student who is now a colleague, taught in urban at-risk schools way before our project. Amanda is a constant source of advice and support. I am grateful for her help and friendship, forever.

Patti Cleary grew from student, to colleague, to friend. She practiced English teaching as it should be practiced and now has a leadership role in education. Patti is one of my guides in this profession.

Several other teachers have inspired me, including Matt Giordano, Laura Harig, Anne Vlosky, and Kathleen Zagar.

My colleague Janet Bean helped me shape my earliest attempts at writing about the project, and I thank Janet for all her help and support.

Paulette U-Rycki is the greatest teacher I have ever met. Her talents, too numerous to mention here, amaze me. She is the great unsung hero of my life. She is an outstanding urban high school teacher, a skill difficult to acquire. Paulette remains in the background but deserves to be honored in ways we reserve for sports stars. Paulette saves lives.

Lynn Waid, a project alumna, has turned into an outstanding city teacher and she may ensure the continuation of this project for the foreseeable future. I am so grateful for our friendship and our continued collaboration.

Greta, my wife, hears about my work every day. Her advice is amazingly objective and thoughtful. She is my best friend and most trusted adviser. Greta tells it like it is. She is loving and tough minded, so I get sound, reliable advice and support. I love her, and I am grateful for her willingness to help me.

Jane and Lizzy, my daughters, are the reasons I go to work in the morning. I look forward to seeing this book on their shelves.

■ Megan's Acknowledgments

In my second semester as a graduate student with no teaching experience and no knowledge about how to be a teacher, I took Hal's Advanced Instructional Techniques course. But this wasn't just any education course. Hal didn't teach me theoretical ways about teaching, make me buy books on teaching methods, or lecture me about how to become a good teacher. Instead, he threw me and my classmates into an urban classroom and let us learn about teaching by giving us opportunities to teach and make mistakes. Like any effective teacher, Hal put me and my fellow teachers-in-training in authentic situations where we were allowed to experiment and practice what we had learned. The Galway project not only benefited the high school kids but also gave us college education students real teaching experiences, so when it came time to do our student teaching, we were a little more prepared. I learned so much about how to become a good teacher by experiencing the power of being placed in Galway's real situations.

I now realize how important courses like Advanced Instructional Techniques are to the education and training of our future teachers. Yet I don't know of any other colleges of education that are offering these kinds of courses to their students. My teaching experiences at Galway far outweigh any course I've taken in my master's program or any other field experience I've gained. Merely observing teachers in action or learning how to make copies doesn't help me become a good teacher. The more practice I have and the more I learn from experienced teachers like Hal and Sally, the more learning becomes meaningful to me.

Thank you, Hal, for giving me the chance to teach real students, formulate my own lessons, and reflect on my mistakes. Your Galway project was my most memorable, fun, educational teaching experience in my entire master's program. If only more professors would get their students involved in real teaching! Think of how many high school and college students could learn from one another. Thank you for your patience, support, and encouragement. I can always count on you for excellent career and life advice. As a teacher now, I look back on our writing sessions and how you treated me not as one of your students, but as one of your friends, and tears fill my eyes. You are my inspiration as a teacher, and I am honored to be your friend. Thank you so much for caring about me and my future.

I went into Hal's graduate assistantship as an English major with the writing habits of an essayist and came out a nonfiction story writer and an enthusiastic English teacher. It's difficult to put into words how grateful I am that Hal has so freely given me the opportunity to write with him. I have a feeling most other professors would have merely mentioned me in the acknowledgments for doing a bit of research or made me do menial tasks so he could publish "his" book. But Hal asked me to write this book with him . . . and he always reminded me that he would not write this book without me. Thank you, Hal, for turning me into the kind of writer I've always dreamed of becoming (I still have a lot to learn, but you gave me a strong foundation), and thank you for giving me this rare opportunity to have coauthored a book at the age of twenty-four. Writing this book with you was the pinnacle of my education and training as an English teacher.

Thank you, also, to the other two "wizards" in my life: Dr. Nicholson, wherever you are, I highly doubt you will ever read this book, but I'll never forget the kind, motivating words you said to me as a freshman in college that helped me realize that I had a love for writing. Dr. Ambrisco, your English classes were so fascinating that I couldn't stop thinking or writing about medieval literature! When I think about the kind of literature discussions I want to create in my future classrooms, I think of your interactive classes, which constantly pushed me to analyze, interpret, and reflect. Every child needs a few wizards in his or her life, and I hope I can be someone's wizard someday.

I also have more than a sneaking suspicion that very few, if any, publishers would have given me, a young graduate student, a book contract. Thank you, Lisa, for seeing Hal's vision in asking me to become a cowriter. Thank you for giving us time and space to write and freedom to write in our own way. Your writing advice was invaluable and impeccable; you challenged us to become better writers, and as a result you have made us proud of our work.

Thank you, Mom and Dad, for your love and support and for all the sacrifices you have made so that your kids could have the best education possible. Even though I was a difficult student in grade school and high school, you always encouraged me to do better. I'm sorry it took me so long to believe in myself and excel in school. While I didn't get the kind of grades you wanted for me during my school years, I believe I was that kind of student for a reason: now I feel like I can motivate the kids I used to be like as a student.

Last, but certainly not least, is my Irish dream. I intended to write this portion in perfect Polish just for you, but I am not as good in Polish as I want to be. However, I can promise you that someday I will be able to freely speak in this beautiful language with you, your parents, friends, grandma, and our baby. Thank you for leaving early that one November night and stopping to meet me on Headford Road in Galway. The only way I can explain that night is to accept that God must love me because somehow, despite all the factors that could have prevented our meeting, we ended up in the right place at the right time. I'm not a big fan of fate, but I think I have to consider that night as the only exception. Thank you for always being my source of optimism, encouragement, support, patience, and love. Although you are not in the field of education, you are my greatest teacher in life. *Ja bardzo kocham ciebie, moj kochany mążu.*

References

Allington, R. 2001. *What Really Matters for Struggling Readers: Designing Research-Based Programs*, 89–110. New York: Addison-Wesley Longman.

Atwell, N. 1998. *In the Middle: New Understandings About Writing, Reading, and Learning*, 2d ed., 148–216. Portsmouth, NH: Heinemann.

Bahl, Portia [pseud.]. 2006. Recorded interview, May 17.

Baines, L., and H. Foster. 2006. "A School for the Common Good." *Educational Horizons* 84 (4): 221–28.

Beers, K. 2003. *When Kids Can't Read: What Teachers Can Do. A Guide for Teachers 6–12*. Portsmouth, NH: Heinemann.

Bloom, B. 1956. *Taxonomy of Educational Objectives, Handbook 1: Cognitive Domain*. New York: Longman.

Broadway, F. 2006. Recorded interview, March 2.

Bruner, J. 2004. *Toward a Theory of Instruction*. Cambridge, MA: Belknap Press.

Centers for Disease Control and Prevention. 2006. Retrieved November 28, 2007 from http.//cdc.gov/ncipc/duip/spotlite/teendrivers.

Daniels, H. 2002. *Literature Circles: Voice and Choice in Book Clubs and Reading Groups*. Portland, ME: Stenhouse.

Darling-Hammond, L. 2000. "New Standards, Old Inequalities: School Reform and the Education of African American Students." *The Journal of Negro Education* 69 (4): 263–87.

Dillon, S. 2007. "Schools Scramble for Teachers Because of Spreading Turnover, Retirements and Stress Shrinking the Pool." *The New York Times*, August 27, A1 and A13.

"Diplomas Count for What? Preparing Students for College Careers, and for Life After High School." 2007. *Education Week* 26 (40): 5.

Draper, S. 1996. *Tears of a Tiger*. New York: Simon Pulse.

Foster, H. 2002. *Crossing Over: Teaching Meaning-Centered Secondary English Language Arts*. Mahwah, NJ: Lawrence Earlbaum Associates.

Foster, H., and I. Newman. 1988. "Error Analysis for High School English Teachers." *Language & Education: An International Journal* 2 (4): 229–38.

Galway High School students [pseud.]. 2006. Recorded interview, May 17.

Gere, A. R., L. Christenbury, and K. Sassi. 2005. *Writing on Demand: Best Practices and Strategies for Success*. Portsmouth, NH: Heinemann.

Gilyard, K. 1991. *Voices of the Self: A Study of Language Competence*. Detroit, MI: Wayne State University Press.

Graves, D. H. 1983. *Writing: Teachers and Children at Work*. Portsmouth, NH: Heinemann.

Greenblatt, S. 2007. Interview, July 13.

Haberman, M. 1991. "The Pedagogy of Poverty Versus Good Teaching." *Phi Delta Kappan* 73 (4): 290–94.

"Highly Mobile Students: Educational Problems and Possible Solutions." 1991. *ERIC Clearinghouse on Urban Education Digest* 73: 1.

Hillocks, G. 1986. *Research in Written Composition*. Urbana, IL: National Council of Teachers of English.

———. 2007. *Narrative Writing: Learning a New Model in Teaching*. Portsmouth, NH: Heinemann.

Johnston, D. C. 2006. "The Ultra-Rich Give Differently From You and Me," *The New York Times*, July 2, 3.

Kagan, D. M. 1980. "Run-on and Fragment Sentences: An Error Analysis." *Research in the Teaching of English* 14 (2): 127–38.

Kershaw, T. 1992. "The Effects of Educational Tracking on the Social Mobility of African Americans." *Journal of Black Studies* 21 (1): 152–69.

King, S. 2000. *On Writing*. New York: Pocket Books.

Kopetz, P. B., A. J. Lease, and B. Z. Warren-Kring. 2006. *Comprehensive Urban Education*. Boston, MA: Pearson.

Kotter, J., and H. Rathgeber. 2005. *Our Iceberg Is Melting: Changing and Succeeding Under Any Conditions*. New York: St. Martin's Press.

Kozol, J. 1991. *Savage Inequalities: Children in American Schools*. New York: Crown.

Krishna, V. 1975. "The Syntax of Error." *Journal of Basic Writing* 1 (1): 43–49.

Ladson-Billings, G. 1999. "Preparing Teachers for Diverse Student Populations: A Critical Race Theory Perspective." *Review of Research in Education* 24 (1): 211–47.

———. 2004. "New Directions in Multicultural Education: Complexities, Boundaries, and Critical Race Theory." In *Handbook of Research on Multicultural Education, Second Edition*, ed. J. Banks and C. Banks. San Francisco: Jossey-Bass.

Lesesne, T. 2003. *Making the Match: The Right Book for the Right Reader at the Right Time, Grades 4–12*. Portland, ME: Stenhouse.

———. 2007. "Making the Match." Speech given at the Literacy Leadership Institute, the National Council of Teachers of English, Charleston, SC, June 25.

McCourt, F. 2005. *Teacher Man*. New York: Scribner.

Moffett, J. 1987. *Teaching the Universe of Discourse*. Portsmouth, NH: Boynton/Cook.

Moll, L. 1992. *Vygotsky and Education: Instructional Implications and Applications of Sociohistorical Psychology*. Cambridge, UK: Cambridge University Press.

National Center for Education Statistics. 2005. *Common Core of Data*. Retrieved February 28, 2006 from http://nces.ed.gov/ccd/.

O'Brien, P. 1993. *Shakespeare Set Free: Teaching* Romeo and Juliet, Macbeth, *and* A Midsummer Night's Dream. New York: Washington Square Press.

Ogbu, J. U. 1990. "Minority Education in Comparative Perspective." *The Journal of Negro Education* 59 (1): 45–57.

Ogbu, J. U., and H. D. Simons. 1998. "Voluntary and Involuntary Minorities: A Cultural-Ecological Theory of School Performance with Some Implications for Education." *Anthropology and Education Quarterly* 29 (2): 155–88.

Ohio Department of Education. 2005. *2004–2005 School Year Report Card*. Retrieved February 28, 2006 from www.ode.state.oh.us/reportcard.

Palacas, A. 2001. "Liberating American Ebonics from Euro-English." *College English* 63 (3): 326–52.

———. 2006. Recorded interview, March 13.

Probst, R. E. 2004. *Response and Analysis: Teaching Literature in Secondary School,* 2d ed. Portsmouth, NH: Heinemann.

Rief, L. 1992. *Seeking Diversity: Language Arts with Adolescents*. Portsmouth, NH: Heinemann.

Romano, T. 2000. *Blending Genre, Altering Style: Writing Multigenre Papers*. Portsmouth, NH: Heinemann.

Russo, P. 2004. "What Makes Any School an Urban School?" *Determining Urban Schools*. Retrieved November 28, 2007 from www.oswego.edu/~prusso1/what_makes_any_school_an_urban_s.htm.

Smitherman, G. 2004. "Language and African Americans: Movin on Up a Lil Higher." *Journal of English Linguistics* 32 (3): 187–96.

———. 2006. *Word from the Mother: Language and African Americans*. New York: Routledge.

Swanson, C. B. 2004. "Who Graduates? Who Doesn't? A Statistical Portrait of Public High School Graduation, Class of 2001." Urban Institute, Nonpartisan Economic and Social Policy Research." Retrieved November 28, 2007 from www.urban.org/url.cfm?ID=410934.

Talbert-Johnson, C. 2004. "Structural Inequities and the Achievement Gap in Urban Schools." *Education and Urban Society* 37 (1): 22–36.

Tatum, A. 2005. *Teaching Reading to Black Adolescent Males: Closing the Achievement Gap*. Portland, ME: Stenhouse.

———. 2007. "Building the Textual Lineages of African American Male Adolescents." In *Adolescent Literacy: Turning Promise into Practice*, ed. K. Beers, R. Probst, and L. Rief. Portsmouth, NH: Heinemann.

Tyson, K. 2003. "Notes from the Back of the Room: Problems and Paradoxes in the Schooling of Young Black Students." *Sociology of Education* 76 (4): 326–43.

Weaver, C. 1996. *Teaching Grammar in Context*. Portsmouth, NH: Boynton/Cook.

Wheeler, R. S., and R. Swords. 2006. *Code-Switching: Teaching Standard English in Urban Classrooms*. Urbana, IL: National Council of Teachers of English.

Index